HANDS *at a* LIVE FIRE

BY THE SAME AUTHOR

Poetry

FOX ON A BARN DOOR

THE SOLITARIES

THE NIGHT BATHERS

GLOVES TO THE HANGMAN

BURNING THE IVY

Children's Verse

THE LION'S CAVALCADE

Fiction

YOU'VE NEVER HEARD ME SING

Autobiography

THE HIGH PATH

HANDS *at a* LIVE FIRE

selected poems

Ted Walker

SECKER & WARBURG
LONDON

First published in England 1987 by
Martin Secker & Warburg Limited
54 Poland Street, London W1V 3DF

British Library Cataloguing in Publication Data

Walker, Ted
Hands at a live fire.
I. Title
821′. 914 PR6073.A4

ISBN 0–436–56120–4

Typeset by Inforum Ltd, Portsmouth
Printed by Redwood Burn Ltd, Trowbridge

TO THE MEMORY OF
MY DEAR WIFE LORNA

ACKNOWLEDGEMENTS

The poems 'By the Saltings', 'Breakwaters', 'Skimmers', 'Estuary', 'The Skate Fishers', 'The Burning', 'By the Bridge', 'Carp', 'Rook Shoot', 'Starlings', 'Mushrooms', 'Heron', 'Homing Pigeons', 'Mules', 'After Fever', 'On Scafell', 'Lemons', 'Sunday Drive to the Beach', 'The Harpooning', 'The Pyttons', 'Grass', 'Journey Back', 'A Place of Trees', 'Swallows', 'Boy by a River', 'A celebration for Autumn', 'After Drought', 'Snow in Southern England', 'Letter to Barbados', 'August', 'Afterwards', 'Vipers,' 'Stanzas for the Graves' and 'Moving' appeared originally in the *New Yorker* (© 1963, 1964, 1965, 1966, 1967, 1968, 1969, 1970, 1971, 1972, 1974, 1975 and 1977 The New Yorker Magazine, Inc.)

Other poems in this volume appeared originally in *Encounter,* the *Observer,* the *Poetry Review,* the *Listener, Priapus,* the *Times Literary Supplement, Stand, Outposts,* the *London Magazine,* the *Transatlantic Review,* the *Critical Quarterly,* the *Spectator,* the *Sunday Times,* the *New York Times,* the *Sunday Telegraph,* the *Boston University Journal* and the *New Statesman.*

Many thanks are also due to the BBC, The Poetry Book Society, The National Book League, The South-East Arts Association, The Arts Council of Great Britain, The Globe Playhouse Trust, The Southern Arts Association, The Borestone Mountain Poetry Awards and P.E.N.

CONTENTS

PART ONE

(Fox on A Barn Door 1965)

PART TWO

(The Solitaries 1967)

PART THREE

The Night Bathers 1970)

PART FOUR

(Gloves to the Hangman 1973)

PART FIVE

(Burning the Ivy 1978)

PART ONE

Fox on A Barn Door

POEMS 1963–4

(For Lorna and our children)

By the Saltings

When the wind is in the thrift
gently, down by the saltings,
at dawn when the vapours lift;

and pattering sanderlings
run from you rather than fly
across the sand flat screaming;

before the runnels drain dry
among the sea-lavender
and sun severs sea from sky;

there is time enough, under
any listing low-tide hull
of your choosing, to wonder

at the force of it to pull
you to its shelter, alone
as you are and as fearful

as some crab beneath some stone.

Breakwaters

Elms are bad, sinister trees.
Falling, one leaf too many,
they kill small boys in summer,
tipped over by a crow's foot,
bored with the business of leaves.

An uneasiness attends
dead elms – timber for coffins,
ammunition boxes. And
breakwaters. Bolts open sores
of orange rust in their flanks,

and yet there is loveliness.
Ultimate green of eelgrass
soothes with the comfort of hair
all the tiny agonies
that crawl in hidden places

and sing when the tide is low
and death is not imminent,
scrabbling in an eczema
of pink and white barnacles
and mussels of midnight blue.

Terrifying as altars
by night, black, a sea-Stonehenge.
Filigrees of little wracks
dance on them at high water
in a devil dance. They change.

Their male look lasts a few tides;
when the reek is washed away
and the stubble is shaven,
on a tall September night
the sea will take his new brides.

In his calm he will lap them,
then batter their waists away,
emphasize their Celtic heads.
And when they are old and raddled,
thin, thin as a Belsen arm,

they will stand bare and skinny
and their stringent, hard old hearts
will disregard his knocking.
Dour, malignant to the core,
they will try to outlive him.

Skimmers

When the sun begins to throw
between boulders darknesses
and the skimmers gather shells
at the edge of amber pools,
he follows his long shadow
through the sea-wall buttresses.

He stands by the longest groyne
in a black and tattered coat,
watching a boy make a mound
of oyster shells on the sand,
hurl them up the wind and on,
curving, curling, lying flat

in the windwall, falling fast
to the dark Decembered bark
that lists by the low-tide mark.
Too old for the skimming now,
still he advises, will boast
of the skill he once had, how

as a boy he used the wind
to lob a cockle over
trees as high as a rook flies.
So he flings his memories
again and again, never
disbelieved. His tales soar and

are caught awhile in the breath
of a boy's brief innocence.
When he comes here wanting death
but not the dying of it,
watching wind in water
white in the seas of winter,

his eyes weep truths of summers
when crops of poppies were blown
like paper parasols back
and wings of yellowhammer
hovered on the white chalk rock.
And when he moves on alone,

shuffling up the pea-beach track
on shores of his mind's making,
he does not stop to look back
at the long rollers breaking;
or at the boy that he knows
at a distance follows.

Estuary

As the image of the sun
after the blinding moment
lasts on the closed lids violet
an instant, and colour comes
across the tight eye's darkness
though the source of light has gone,

so when I take the low lane
between the fields of barley,
with the slither of a sea-
wind sucking the sun-cracked husks,
to gaze at the sunken hulks
of ships as they flake at noon

in the lapped inlet, I can
recall that, with the tide-race
of boyhood just begun, once
I ran down the jetty steps,
stubbing up pebbles, and stopped
to stare at a bark broken

in three across the open
mudflat, each part with a mast
still and splintering spars, fast
in banks of sand: and though I
remember the terror my
eyes saw treading the decks on

that bright morning with the wind
light now – the wind that had smashed
that great ship fallen, awash
like driftwood, ribbed in fitful
patches of water – yet still
I would wish to be alone

with the loneliness of then;
and free to make my horrors
walk the boards beyond the shore
at the bidding of my will
only; with the power, as well
as to make, to efface them

by turning to see the men
with bright bandana faces
gladdening the noonday as
they picked the purple winkles
like scatterings of damsons
with salt dried like bloom on them.

Porpoises

Sometimes in summer the sea
looks infrangible; dull steel
dimpled like a dinner-gong.
The metal may be pitted
at the far rim with the hulk
of a forty-foot basker.

A sudden clap-trap of gulls –
and mackerel-magnetized
the sea scribbles lines of force
to attract crazed porpoises
frantic with feeding and rut
close to an inshore bather.

The cow gives suck as she rolls
through her bull's parabola,
dragging her calf over groynes
in his wake of white lather:
and her broad, round head tumbles
to his rhythm. Her thick lips

curl like a negress's lips.
When she dives her flukes lie poised
on the surface an instant
as she breaks another back
among the perfervid shoal
with an automatic snap

of appalling, fluted jaws.
The herd is sleek and wanton,
frenzied, intent as athletes;
paced by herring, hulls of ships,
they never stop, never sleep.
They copulate on the move.

And sometimes, along the shore,
you come across one stranded
like a great, obscene, black slug.
Age, exhaustion, impotence,
but no disease can kill them.
They die when they fall behind.

The Skate Fishers

Now, as at its first shining,
Saturn burns slow and alone
to rise on a sudden night
in time for a tide neaping
to an imminent full moon,
they come to their boats and light

their lamps. Propitious the sound
of the suck and the gunwale's
rough rub on the quay-wall stone,
the dry deck strewn with dry sand,
no wind fingering it nor swells
to roll one grain away. Then

offshore, no boards creaking, still
amid stillness of sea,
the long throb of engines stopped,
they must wait a while till
indigo water and sky
violet have interlocked.

Nine such nights a year only
they have, and some must be missed,
when they may pay a line low
to the grey scabbed skate that lie
among the boulders buttressed
in, nine nights only to pay

a long line down at the mark
that needs such calm to be found
and held. But when the ratchet
clatters, when a kittiwake
disturbed rises, when, entwined
in weed, line hisses, at that

taut instant the great skate dives
through his black rock canyon
deep, deep, beating his wide wings
on its walls; on, on through caves
of no man's knowing. Upon
some arcane ledge, huge, he hangs

pulsing with irritation.
And with each heave of him pumps
the rod above and sideways,
fretting the tightened line on
a jutting shelf till it snaps.
The men, like petrels, restless,

move on across the surface,
veined and broken, through the stars'
shattered images to shore;
and the skate, with a grimace
of torn lip, spits blood, and goes
to do a killing elsewhere.

On the Sea Wall

Attending the First Coming,
expecting that some shudder
of Him should pulse here under
me stronger than the knocking
sea that throbs through the greenheart,
I wait for a faith to start
shaking me. Again nothing

stirs. But I stay, lest I miss
beyond the mind's wall, where are
distances that never star
was adequate to express,
some comet fall of insight
in the chasm of this night
to light me my loneliness.

Conger

An hour since, you lay coiled in your inheritance:
The broken spars of a sunken Spanish orange-boat,
The manor you won when you weighed a mere forty
pounds.
There you lived alone, eating all spies and intruders,
Hidden down among the cold, chryselephantine stones.

You have teeth like the spikes on a barrel-organ drum:
That necrologic gape closed its horny doors of knives
On the hebete like the Iron Maid of Nuremberg.
You have the limbless streamlining of the latest cars.
Your tiny scales are apt, like a wrestler's tiny eyes.

Now you lie dead. On the bottom boards you lie dead.
This is how things should be.

Under the Pier

He has a bargain who buys
the cheap, comfortable lies
they are selling on the pier.

Inside the Hall of Mirrors
you can buy cut-price horrors:
little men with chorea

will dance for you. The Ghost Train
always brings you back again
from Hell. And you're always near

an emergency exit.
You're entitled to forget
crude facsimiles of fear –

you pay to. It's free down here
to look at the old dead-beats
who lie embalmed in their sweat

without will enough to leer
at the couples doing what
they can against the wall. Not

an urge left in them, they're
waiting till it's time to go;
they'd die, but don't know how to.

This is how things are. Nothing's
unnatural that happens.
They lie in the night and hear

the barkers up on the pier
cry dummy death for the tasting.
Down here the kicks are lasting.

Harvest Moon

Wafer of altar-bread, the moon,
white, round, brittle at the edge.
In a wisp of fibre soon
September-priest takes bread; at ledge
of sky, the chalice lip, in flood
of sunrise dips the moon in blood.

Erosion

There have been
such times before; times when rain
has seemed ceaseless and the clay
has slipped like this, endlessly
away.

We have known
days like these when it seemed sun
would come alien to our eyes
if again it came to us
as once:

when we hoped,
when at last the rains had stopped,
we would learn some way to bear
the weight of so much water;
endure

one more time
if it came, and it has come,
the sight of the sodden clay
as it slips like this, endlessly
away.

The Burning

The stubble burning began
today, fire tonguing furrows
where lately the rats had run
that now, with pheasant and gull,
skulk among rusting harrows
at field-edge out of the pull

of funnelled winds. With the flames'
peremptory signatures
to the season's ending came
a flaked ash of cirrus wisp
tonight, multiple fractures
of yellow trees, a last wasp

kindled in the hips, berries
that cracked in the red spindles
and a thin wind that carries
yet detonations of jays'
wings as the last light dwindles
below the branch-line of yews.

And in the burning fields now
the images are changing.
Sometimes the fires are a row
of children's sunlit faces,
round, in yellow hair tumbling;
or, as a night breeze rises

on a sudden, a saw edge
surging jagged through the straw,
ripping from hollow to ridge
a whole furlong. Tomorrow
will come plovers and jackdaw
flocks to pick a living through

the desolate acres. Oaks,
leafless, will be as thumb-prints
smudged on the sky; rains will soak
each last, cold cinder away.
A sense of panic, no plants
left to grow, strengthens as clay

sweats, cooling. I would wish
the fires to burn a while more,
fruits not to fall from the bush
a while more, nor I to pass
by, till the slate-shine shives are
cut for the coming of ice.

By the Bridge

I recall, before the banks
sank in this wilderness of rains,
clear waters of the Wild Brooks
torrented atop white rocks
worn smooth and slabbed, with a sun
in bubbles splintered over them.

I stood on this bridge and saw
the waters mix; the confluence,
too, of sparrows and shadow
the length of the long hedgerow;
and finches strung on fences
like bright beads on an abacus.

There were sounds of quietness
not listened for, but heard
among beds of watercress
where, with eyes of gentleness
and hocks sucking soft hot mud,
some patient herd always waded.

Every close-cropped pasture, lush
with marsh-marigold, was quiet
with an intermittent hush
of leaves in a delicate ash
when the wind unentwined
and not a cricket fidgeted.

Whatever the stream bore down
from unaccountable hills
in the misted distance, passed on
to gaze at dark reflections
in the deep blue calm of pools
below the drop of the falls.

All ugliness, all violence
passed away. Through the stone piers
of the bridge's permanence,
uprooted trees in remonstrance
brushed eely green streamers
of silkweed, pulled to the weir

beyond. Even when the great storm
broke, massive banks drained
vast cargoes away; but a dam
of blackened branches jammed
across the stream and all poured
over. Still the lands lie under flood

and no quietness of sound
is heard now in the silence
seeping from the vanished ground.
Violated, broken things find
islands to rot upon. The dance
of the multiple suns is done.

Carp

By day falls the white blossom
of may on his olive back
inert on top like a rock.
Small silver shiners spin from
him as bright jangles of fry
veer from his stillness. But by

night, when bats bring their darkness
and start to sip at the pool
in a sideslip as they whirl
round the same two trees endlessly, come the night skirmishes.
He has been waiting for this.

It is as though night prises
a scale or two up. He bolts
through reeds to smoothen them; halts;
sucks the yellow irises
encrusted with yellow eggs.
He sucks till his belly sags,

as he quaffs in unison
with the cows' rough tongues ripping
grass at the edge. His sipping
admits a long procession
of passing flies. Then it stops.
He turns within his length, flaps

a gossamer from his fin,
and, exploiting his great strength,
hurls his amplitude the length
of a pond too small for him,
back and back and back again,
savaging the restriction

of lily stalks and the roots
where the lurking yellow perch
hover in amazement, arch-
ing their spines. And he starts
circuiting, circuiting, like
a brash skater at a rink,

trailing his barbels beneath
his gape as he goes, rejoic-
ing that he was made for this
alone, until the first breath
of a day breeze blows and quietly he attends a new night.

Grebe

Today the April winds blow
in the tippets of your crest;
the waves are hard beneath you,
as by your will. And you stand
wide-winged like a little Christ
using the water like land.

I can forget the mammal
that I am for days; and though
in the womb I was reptile,
fish, I have no memory
of the scales I shed, and no
sense of the gekko in me.

But you – are you going back
to be again what once you were
before your ancestors shook
their first wet feathers and flew
into the alien air
you find so alien now?

Cuckoo-pint

So cold now. I remember
you – bright hedgerow tarts you were,
flagrant in your big red beads,
cheerful, vulgar and brazen.
But then,

in a sudden October,
when the white night of winter
came, you put aside your gauds
and took vows. Now you open
again,

hooded, cool and sinister.
I know you for what you are
unveiled: loose, secular brides
frustrated with this convent
torment.

Rook Shoot

Against the evening light, strung
across banks of cumulus,
goitres of mistletoe hung
from the necks of poplars.
Higher, in elms, rookeries
knotted the topmost traceries,
rank and black like a cancered lung.

Always a restlessness turned
in the tops of those tall trees:
even at rest the birds leaned,
lurching backwards as a breeze
blew fitful into their faces
scabrous with the rub of branches
jabbed. There was no comfort

up in those crowded tenements,
save the warmth sometimes of sun
cupped in Aprilled-out softness
of new leaves, barely green,
that soothed for a while the roughness
away. At a time of this
tenderness, the men came.

Quickly they did what they had
come to do. They had no need to kill,
but some part of them remembered
the need of a man to kill
and had brought them with their want
under the purple birds. They shot.
And one by one the dark parcels fell,

thudding, to cumber the ground
underfoot, twitching out the last
frenetic beat of wing and heart.
We, when the men had passed
on, stood a while to watch
some turning birds in the distance
gyrate nearer, nearer, land

indomitable under
the ravage, walk among
the spilt eggs, peck them, gather
sustenance enough to sing
a cracked, ragged song up in
the roomier trees, to begin
tomorrow a new growth all over.

Disused Canal

Earth began to take it back
years, years before men left
it; and their horses, put to pasture,
trailed their manes in the softness of fern fronds; years, before
their long, brass-bound barges sank
to glint among the kingcups.

No sooner were they opened
for the first time, these locks –
and the only rush ever
of a wall of water shook
each bridge, quiet over
stagnancy since – than dormant
seeds in the clay bed sprouted,

never to be put down, bled
once a year and strengthened by
bill-hook. The hold tightened;
banks grew close with tufty
hummocks. Then rose the silted
bottom through the water and
once again the land won back

the length of cut. A thick
scum of duckweed only lies
where a man might have stood once,
and still have drowned. Only flies,
with the drug of dusk, now dance
to an oriental music
where the bargees sang to the hooves,

There are places where no weed moves
ever, now, when a wind blows:
there will come a time, and soon,
for the shrivelling of willows
and for the last flocks of down
to toss like gondolas on waves
from a swan's swooping. And

when the final crumb will have dried
and the fissures of June have scarred
parched patches where no grass
will grow, they will come once more,
the men, to turn back earth
encrusted with the sun and wind,
hard as they and as obdurate.

Terrains Vagues

At the edge of any town
and the edge of any life
are tracts we never build on;
ragged wildernesses, half-
wild, unkempt and overgrown.
They're easy to return from

and there is no risk. Children,
gipsies, lovers, tramps, all go there
to do what they must: and none
can come to harm, save when we're
there too. For we infect them
with our coming. When we stare

at them, steal a turf or two,
litter them with what we've felt,
they are soiled by what we do
and they watch us with our guilt.

Starlings

Our fears, like starlings, gather
with the dusk. Small particles
they come, innumerable,
flying direct from further
skies of mind only guessed at.
Wheeling, they circle us, squat

near. If ever a pair of birds
should strut a sunlit pavement
before us, caught in movement
of the day's concern, we goad
them, approach, put them to flight;
sometimes, even, feed them. But

lodged, untouchable by night,
in the high clerestories
of the stone-still, moon-carved trees
we move among, they will not
be put up at our passing
boldly under their roostings.

Sometimes we can keep away
through the long-lain night. Awake
we may avoid them, though flocks
heave throbbing through our dreams, high
in the misproportioned limbs
of our imaginings.

If we should decide to come
to them, hear their mummeries
mock us when one of them stirs
to ripple through all of them,
sacristan black, we may judge
their strength, though they will not budge

before the day. When they go
they leave uneasy calm, as
they turn as one like louvres,
letting the sunlight through.
And only the sense remains
of the black beneath the sheen

and the knowledge that the swift
and silent flight of other
birds, unseen, has passed over
us, sinister, borne aloft
by wings more menacing
yet than those of the known starling.

Mushrooms

By three spindle-trees, far from
the far stars once in a dream,
in a dream I stood alone
beneath a varicose moon
that hung by the Little Wood
still. And though no wind had blown

that night, yet the bulrushes
swished and the parching grasses,
sibilant with the hustle
of dry vipers, were alive
with scales. I ground the pestle
of each tree-top as I moved

into the moon's mortar, fled
through aspens where fear quivered
me still from the lisping fields,
until, exhausted, I fell
among mushrooms and lay cold
with the shudder of them all

about me. I watched them grow
with a shuffle of mould through
dead leaves, taking the colour
of the night that conceived them,
pink and brown in the pallor
of a falling-flecked moonbeam,

black in the shadow of roots.
And in that flicker of plants,
only the nightshade I knew
by name, knew that its berries
would fall and die where they grew
and poison drain away. Those

other growths – unkillable,
teeming coolie-caps, fungal
infections on an oak-bark,
all the fine spores that I breathed
that night – live on in the dark
wildernesses of my mind,

and they will lie a long age
inactive there till I reach
once more and unwillingly
those three spindle-trees far from
sleep – trees that once before I
saw in a dream, in a dream.

Easter Poem

I had gone on Easter Day
early and alone to be
beyond insidious bells
(that any other Sunday
I'd not hear) up to the hills
where are winds to blow away

commination. In the frail
first light I saw him, unreal
and sudden through lifting mist,
a fox on a barn door, nailed
like a coloured plaster Christ
in a Spanish shrine, his tail

coiled around his loins. Sideways
his head hung limply, his ears
snagged with burdock, his dry nose
plugged with black blood. For two days
he'd held the orthodox pose
The endemic English noise

of Easter Sunday morning
was mixed in the mist swirling
and might have moved his stiff head.
Under the hill the ringing
had begun: and the sun rose red
on the stains of his bleeding.

I walked the length of the day's
obsession. At dusk I was
swallowed by the misted barn,
sucked by the peristalsis
of my fear that he had gone,
leaving nails for souvenirs.

But he was there still. I saw
no sign. He hung as before.
Only the wind had risen
to comb the thorns from his fur.
I left my superstition
stretched on the banging barn door.

PART TWO

The Solitaries

POEMS 1964–5

(For my mother and father)

Crocuses

Walking in the walled garden
of our life, sometimes we stop
by beds of blue, broken
crocuses where, as children,
we loved to watch the petals drop.

Recalling we were glad
once, glad with the sparrows
rampaging April away – suffered
such wanton wings to burst
first flowers that are our sorrows

now – we scan that long monotony
of level lawn, our tended
sward of years. Each daisy
we remember, ruthlessly
grubbed up; those drifts we raked

of wind-scorched blossom, black as snow
melting on winter water.
So, before our brooms burn through
the smash of bloom that springs ago
we left the wind to scatter,

briefly we pause: regret
the vacant seemliness
by which we live. For which we lost
that proper, vital gift of waste
whereby the one-day crocus dies.

Clouds

I had a mind to tell you of them all,
My son, the figures in the clouds that sped
As I thought only for me in the sky

Of my childhood; of the mane round the snarl
Of a lion's tossing head, or the head
Holed with sunshine eyes of Christ in glory;

Great maps of Japan, with wisp of atoll
Lone in a Pacific else uncharted.
I'd tell you, but the clouds have blown away

That I saw pictures in, that I might say
Were harp and trumpet, fiddle and cymbal;
That in my dreaming afterwards I played

Upon to angels they became, slowly
In all space riding the clouds they were . . . till
My opening eye saw them no more, dimmed

In the flicker of passing truths that I,
With all my unwisdom, too often tell
You of. And so, instead, I have a mind

To hear you tell of likenesses you find
In skies of wonderment you watch for me;
Because I know that you can see them still,

Maps, lions, angels, instruments, Christ's head:
And know you need not lie, as I should lie,
To tell of figures that may last a while

More, for you a while more, before the cloud
You see into will settle in your eye
And you see nothing, taught to see too well.

The Brothers

Winter was probable the August
I was nine. The leaning pipes
of tank-traps slobbered wet rust
at the end of our garden,
letting easterlies in from the sea.
I had had a month, perhaps,
out of the hug of Thermogene:
but now on my bed again
I crouched four-square for the heavy
brother of my asthma. I sobbed
at draughts by the window-jamb
and suffered the rising tide to toss
its rice in fistfuls at the sea-green glass.

I would have said how the swan
had walked into the mine-field,
almost treading on its own
toes. But my voice was only a wire
whizzing thinly in an unused air
as I heard my mother far
across the house, banking the fire
with hacked, masculine jarrah
from the shipyard. Soon my father,
in a black sash of bicycle tyre
salvaged for heeling winter boots,
stepped carefully up our path. Jack's
going to be late, he said. He sat
whistling by my bed, in his socks,
and cut across buckling rubber.

They went on sipping tea
through the moments of explosion;
high water was always meddling
with the mines tidily hidden
in the shingle; there was no novelty,
listening for air-borne jetsam.
But, choking on sacks of empty
feathers the bang was strewing in my mind –
smashed enamel particles of beak,

shreds of black, rubbery web –
I left untouched the dainty slices
of my breathing, I vomited
air, fell slack with thoughts of eyes.

Then, easier, I saw my father's tears
come sudden after the knock;
man's tears, terrible, miraculous
as diamonds. Now Jack. Now Jack,
rare in the starry clover
as his other brother dead
among the sand by Tobruk.
And with a cautious husbandry of grief,
he would not let me see between
the moistened horn of his fingers,
but had me sleep in my ampler breathing,
a whine, a sighing of swan's wings
strengthening nearer into the night.

Heron

He comes down to the shadow
that he left in the shallow
last night. Imperturbable,
pickerel in their stations
barely shift, invulnerable
with him. His feet know these stones.

There are other ways than this:
there are ways only he knows.
In a rickyard where rats are
he could circle, coil his neck,
and with wings at the trail, thrash straw
and spike what he cared to spike.

And there will happen a time
once more for the cheap, random
kill; for striding dikes in March,
rictus agape, wanton, lewd
with his swagger in some ditch,
randy for the taste of toad.

That is for spring. Lethargy
attends easy victory
now. He would slump on his glut,
lumpish with sloth, his wings
lifting, if they lifted, to a flight
without the rhythms of once.

So, while the painted Carolina
duck squat in sets, like china
on the calico water
of dawn, a thick glaze of sleep
on them, the great grey hoarder
of his want, ravening, keeps

the tensile shadow of neck
in readiness round the rock
under him. And, ignoring
the trees where woodpeckers drum
out his hunger, bides, waiting
for the shoal he knows will come.

With Weasel
for John Cotton

Crevice of a soft-rot wall,
the rib-cage of a carcase,
stump crumble, a kingfisher's hole –
anywhere housing foulness
suits. Once from a hulk of pike

one gnawed, eeled up a bank,
wriggling from lust of throat
in a jubilee of stink:
and I, less than owl to it
(packs can attack a man,

in living memory have done),
lay prone to the bulge-eyed
comer from carrion,
wanting him; furrier's remnant,
perfect, desirable scrap. Mine,

I thought, mine, dapper Capone;
I'll scrag the gangster out
and stretch him for his ermine.
I could see where the first cut
'd come, the little nick.

where the white of him was pink,
by his ear pursing. But forgot,
my fingers forking him, his neck
was nothing through a slit
of fence, never mind hot skin –

and up my cuff for a ravin
of blood he was, plundering
elbow, shoulder and armpit; in
darkness, inebriate, drinking
me . . . Bleeding out of suck's reach

I ran profusely out of his touch
from a sloughed heap of coat,
infested with such a stench
that I sensed him all that night
and the next and the next. And though

I burned all my clothes, no
fire could cauterize him out:
for under an ointment, slowly, all my wounds would shut
over him, over him, tight

as any soft-rot wall.

Ox

His fodderer has gone.
He is left to his cud, alone
with a want in his loins.

He prongs a night stagnant
with lolling, warm and dank
with his wish. Fragments

of memory persist
of a time he was lost
in a similar mist:

when he heard the lowing
beyond fields of his knowing
of a heifer, willing

him away. He charged a hedge,
barely flinched as his haunch
was rasped by a branch;

battered till the strop
of his tail passed the gap
and he learned what to gallop

was. In a new darkness
he bellowed off the press
of his loneliness;

ran. Lit with lapwings,
ran; urged with whinnyings,
ran till the thickening

sea-mist overspilt beaches
to swallow the breath of his
lure. Hours, hours, round the reaches

of dismay he wandered,
slowing, till he stumbled
down to sleep. And he dreamed.

In his dream within a dream
he knew why the call had come
to him: but now, in this same

meadow, when memory
returns with mist, thinly
first, then burning like barberry

in the hedgerow glowing
in a night of no star's showing,
no, nor moon, nor lowing

in the air, his eyes are white
with bewilderment.
Not knowing what thing he must

do, only that it must be done,
until the mist has risen
he will run, he will run.

On Scafell

Beyond the last gate, where I made my first halt,
The last of darkness still clung on the rock
Though a ladder of sun leaned on a further mountain.
The valley below was a vellum of mist
For all of August's hung thunder among it.
Glad for rest, I watched – refuting the cold
That carried in the shifting damp of the air –
A buzzard rise slowly over the steaming peat.
Mine, else, the mountain was, whose skylarks
Slept, hidden in the wax and shrub of bilberry.
Beyond the long bog I was to cross, no sheep
Moved in a mesh of black runnels. Water,
The very water was dazed, fumbling, unpurposeful.

Once I had left it behind, the formality
Of standing a moment alone on top of England
Would take an hour, no more. But for the buzzard,
Lazing just within sight on a ledge of wind,
I might have claimed as mine, as won there and then
That total, boundless tundra of solitude
I came before dawn to be on the mountain for.
With his sort of eye I watched him, cairn by cairn,
Rug by rug of shrivelling and emptied carcase.
My shoulders felt how flicking a blunt wing
Sufficed to steady the sun or to turn a rock face;
Fingers warmed as they would had I held him
Shot in all the amazement of his needless beauty.

Once begun, the final pitch, my back to slab
For a mooring against the thrown stacks of gust,
My calves flexed from the nudge of my wondering
Whether any flinching creature could keep there
And not be torn across the insubstantial rock,
Hurled to the grit-faced crags of the wind:
To go on, on into the mountain's shifting now,
On, or back, would have been to ride lightning.
And into the afternoon I kept to a crouch,
A whitened gristle of ravelled fear, mindless
Of wonder, beauty, desire or of solitude,
Being the wind's thing, helpless as the mountain,
A harsh, dry rattle assembling within my craw.

Homing Pigeons

Among left trucks, mailbags, churns,
sometimes in Sunday depots
we glimpse, through dirt-pearled windows
of a stopping train, square wicker
crates, crammed with homing pigeons.
We keep afloat a feather

of memory blown to the air
of our drab compartment.
Singly, over open sea, sheer
from our instrumented course,
we have watched them, confident
beyond their wings' will, cross.

And have thought, outward bound
in sunshine, of the attic
loft where they always land,
their fanciers waiting, alone.
All their lives are goings-back
From places where they have not flown.

Alien they seem. Yet
in their brief apportionment
of flight – a timed parole –
is sensed that homing force that drives
us back from any fanciful
hovering beyond our lives.

For there are wants kept caged on roofs
of the mind's tenements
that coo for us through the dusk,
always hungering, their ruffs
up. They strut their insistence
till we bring them all they ask:

so little; grain enough
to soothe them through the night
they will roost out in sleep.
Or multiply in. If,
neglectful, we forget
their feed, they grate the coop

floor, madden for full crops
and flight. We must indulge
their greed, let them fatten
as they will, some perhaps
surfeiting till they gorge
their death. But few. And in

those interims between
living as we seem to be
and dreaming what we are,
we come to the cage, unseen.
We stroke them as they crowd the wire
while we fumble for the key,

then loose them to the corridor
we trust them to, of sanctioned air.
Vigilant, we watch them take
turn after turn above us till,
wheeling on the thread of our will,
they clatter back in the hanging dark.

Mules

for Leslie Norris

In warm war sun they erupt
in frontier towns, hard-
hoofed in a dark cobbled yard,
waiting for what is apt:
cartridge cases, cordite, shells.

Always the sight of them compels
the memory of what we are.
A newsreel of a distant war
that flickers in our room recalls
a savage, wasting sense in us;

eyes that stare from skirmishes
a continent away propound
the pith of life our lives have dulled.
A braying in the silences
beyond those Asian leaves betrays

some close, restless agency,
half-detected, feared, unseen
in unfamiliar terrain,
marauding, like the lurking spy
that snipes us from the wilderness

of dreams. We know ourselves wise,
mastering violence; but sometimes,
dimly, we sense other wisdoms –
he totally lives who dies
imminently; *those eyes*

only that see with terror see.
We do not say we would have gone
gladly, scrabbling screes to melon-
smelling foothill towns to be
quickened with fear; nor would these

wide-eyed soldiers fail to lob
grenades at the sniper's nest:
it will be time enough to test
our doctrines when our cancers throb.
But, as we watch the mules trot past,

we muse on how, in times of peace,
their withers twitch to flies
as, listlessly, they laze
neglected in corrals, or pace
at tether, shabby and unkempt.

Cowman

Moonlight thickens in the rheum
tacky in my lids. My years
stare me out now, nights. The boom
of heifers loose with the stars
stirs me. I must go to them.

Once, my father had a son
To mend the fences, hurdle
them from harm. I am alone
and glad sometimes to huddle
in a stall till calving's done.

They will be at the brook now,
drinking moonskim. Listen, look,
this is my byre, my meadow;
my father planted this oak
and left me to watch it grow.

They never wander far. Far
ago, far, my son was born
the night he died. Remember,
remember. With the longhorn
I was. I pulled the limber

bull-calf out of her that lived.
I love them wading with such moon.
That was the year I paved
the yard, chiselled in the stone
his name. Him I might have loved.

Hark to them. Fifty-odd
winters together we were,
helping, both, to fill the bed
against the damp. They took her
away, left me to my herd.

Not a day now but the moss
picks out a flint; the coping
soaks up wet and the thatch sags.
My father's tree needs lopping.
I wait for May and new grass.

Founder

I awoke as rushes hissed,
brushing my dream. The stem
fouled the roots of a fig tree.
A day, a night and a day
went by. Nobody came.
We waited. My runt twin wept.

Then there were fangs at my nape.
I was trailed through fallen figs,
meadow-marsh, and up to stone
that, moonlit, I crawled upon
till she brought him and her dugs:
all the strength I had to sap.

He had to be kept alive
long enough to be of use;
when our foster-mother died
I let the woodpecker feed
him, and the shepherds, sometimes.
He worked; cleared an olive grove,

hewed great stones and trimmed them;
laid them as I commanded.
He leaped my wall – but *Romule,*
noli, noli, Romule,
he moaned before I murdered
him. I looked over Latium,

alone, and saw above my hills
an eagle rising like a sun
to burn upon Liguria,
Picenum and Calabria,
turn, and glide superbly down
to strut along my city walls.

Birthday Song

With winds that strop on little stones
Beside the water's open throat,
A steel November birthday hones
The rusted scissors of the thought
That I am thirty and that I
Have yet to see somebody die.

Had I but asked, when I was young,
To touch my sister's hardened hand
(That three-week sister with one lung,
Whose life I could not comprehend),
I may have learned to look on death
As triumph in the fight for breath:

Or if, successive mournings since,
I'd seen a misted mirror clear,
Perhaps my mind could countenance
That life is all we have to fear,
Believing lips set in repose
Suggest far less than I suppose.

For, walking where the river's lip
Is wiped by willows that entwine,
Recalling coffin-slings that slip
Through knuckles knowing more than mine,
I look behind my silent tread
And blink as, level with my head,

My birthday morning mints a sun –
A coin to double-lid an eye
That might, before I'm thirty-one,
Secure the image lastingly
Of how a loved one did not look
Before the last time she awoke.

Experience

Could not predict
    What might have grown,
But had I picked
    What I had sown

There may have been
    Lush fruit to taste,
Would not have seen
    My land laid waste:

But I am glad
    The leaves turned black.
The seed was bad.
    I ploughed it back.

Clay

This land, look, sunk now,
and all the gulls gone,
so soon since the plough.

A dun monotone
glims where the share shone
reds from the furrow.

We who watch her know
we are the next crops
and shall have our use:

when we cease to grow
she will exact us.
We notice how,

as the light subsides,
such as there still is
of sun dribbles in

our footprints. The cliffs
our heels made begin
already crumbling.

Earth, consuming our
small imprints on her,
heals every lesion;

soon our intrusion
will be sucked under.
We know her sanction.

While we watch, wordless,
the turned earth settles
like a new-filled grave.

Listen, a flint shifts.
Though we know we have
not moved, our shadows move.

Pumpkins

Hot in a shade of green
and Brazilian blue
they swell half-hidden, seen
in segments that a few
wasps always walk.

Moist, cobra-head leaves pin
us with blighted eyes, sway
unshunnable in sun
and suck our sight away,
uncoiling stalk

and long, rank rope of stem
from unfathomably
deep beginnings. Scales shine,
the length of them, of dew.
When, with a shake

of fiercer growth, sudden
with warmth and ecstasy
of swelter, some swollen
lolling globes roll to lie,
yellow and pink,

ready for rot, upon
another's oozings, we
must watch. For, seeing them
sever themselves and die
in languor, thick

rind fissured at the seam
and crawling already
with an attendant swarm,
we sense that the heady
and wilful suck

of the plant's oblation
was not to fructify,
simply; but to have done
at last with earth, to dry
after the soak

of it, to seep again
to nothingness. To be
no more, once having grown,
is all they need, and we,
of getting back.

Moths

When there is fog they come,
the solitaries, some
who pass your door and then
turn and pass and turn again.

They linger with harm in them
underneath the streetlamp's hum;
criminal with loneliness
they sip the evening yellowness

sifting from the evening windows
still uncurtained. Wish follows
wish across the darkened grass
striped with paths of light from glass

so thinly separating you
from what the watchers want to do.

And so you rise, turn off the light,
hoping that the darkness might
warn off the settling mothmen who
will look for other lamps to fly to:

or, perhaps, you draw the curtain,
sit an hour or two uncertain
whether or not you heard a footstep,
whether or not you heard it stop,

whether you would hear it again
treading softly in your garden.
Else, you leave your house, your room,
its lightened loneliness, and come

to windows lit with solaces
for you, and us, the solitaries.

Raid

Swastika leaflets had been found
by labourers along the lanes
fresh from the sky those first war dawns.
We bartered copies to pass around;
some of us learned to read from them.
Trees were dropping manifestos
of declaring autumn; rooks rose

ach as the earlier evenings closed
and we went home to our comics.
We spelled out words in italics
that, yelled in the shelters, amazed
our teachers: *das ist verboten,*
Engländer; *alles in Ordnung,*
Herr Kommandant; *Achtung, Achtung!*

We bandied the brittle fragments,
crisp to the lips as new leaf-
falls to the foot, till our throats were rough
with unaccustomed consonants
cracking like twigs. Too young
to understand we might be occupied,
we learned an occupation army's tongue.

They never came. Strange then, that heard
twenty-five autumns on, those phrases
half-forgotten – like notices
yellowing, pinned to a board
in a derelict Nissen hut –
should menace indelibly now. And that, when
September days draw in again,

we should spend remaining summer's silence
equipping for an indiscriminate fall.
Adding to our store of language
a smattering of middle age,
we know some Luftwaffe reconnaissance
still drones towards our placid lives,
spying on our children, us, our wives.

After Fever

Late the third night it was the fever lifted.
I felt composure fall like heavy velours,
fold, fold upon fold, until the room was filled.

Unaware once more of taking any breath
I wiped my breath away from the misted glass
to watch my image outside in the darkness

staring steadily back across the stillness
and into the swaddled air. Here, hours before,
counting each gasp and desperate fingerhold

three hundred feet above slithering ocean,
I clawed the greasy tiles of a sloping roof
and then was launched in a vivifying wind

to learn how easeful falling through water is.
Endlessly, endlessly, cushioned on the plush
that covered what seemed like comfortable death

I felt myself fall till I sensed that the sea
was not sea, nor wind wind, nor this death my death:
and the notion, like my image, vanishing

with the nap of dark in the beginning day
left me standing cold to breathe by a window,
watching the world unstifled with common wind

shuffling back like an ageing adulterer,
traipsing shabbily back through the fallen leaves
and up to my door as if nothing had happened.

Father's Gloves

Not garments. A craftsman's armour
Worn to blunt the hooks of pain.
Massive, white asbestos mitts
He brought back from the shipyard
Hang cool by his blowlamp
And his sailmaker's palm.
In his hearth, treasured still,
Scored by remembered cinders,
Lie gauntlets from his dirt-track days
That sometimes, when his fire is dull,
He wears to prod the embers.
Keeping them rekindles him.

He keeps them all, the pairs
We give him on his birthdays,
Crammed in drawers too full to shut.
Some of them may have a use
At family ceremonial:
But, christening or funeral,
Pigskin, suede, kid or calf,
We'd have him carry them, because
His hands are warmer with them off.

Apocalypse on the Jetty

Weather-rucked, intermittent
in the jetty's starboard light,
the faces of the codling men,
grim, furred with frost, intent,
clamp upon the coming night.

After the last, curling cast,
they trim their tackle, settle
themselves to the searchless lust
that clings to them after a kill.
As the tide slackens, and the shoal

moves on, they know their need.
When day shelves, before full dark,
they drowse to cold in shallows
deep enough to dream in, where they
drift, bait for the want that swallows

them, strafing, as a seeking shark
sucks mullet. January
lifts no lid. They will not wake,
though ice prise open an eye,
before sleep unbars one glimpse

of that long, white-ribbed corridor,
fragrant with wax of ambergris
and lit with pins of phosphor
where, willing Jonahs, alone
beyond all ends of ocean,

they would wish to walk in calm,
their shriek left in the gull's tough jaw.
And, before some morning wakener
lifts their welded fingers from
the tightening grip of their dream –

before they stamp back warmth and fear
to suffuse their bodies once more,
and they return, shivering, home
from the sea's ascendancy
so nearly shared – they will have seen

fragments enough of a vision
that will surely bring them back,
failing, where they will fail again,
to court the comfortable cold
a man might gently die in.

Elegy for a Trotliner

I remember him. Even then,
when we were boys, he looked too worn
to weather out the season
of those winter afternoons
that rasped away the marram dunes.

He used to bring a ball of sun
to dribble from his fork's curled tines
and rinse away; already, often,
half a moon hung like a husk
from fingers of a tamarisk.

All the shingle, seeping, sang
with lives the sea had left the dusk;
intermittently bell-buoys rang
to smaller swells, more faintly, listing
one by one to breakers basting

them where they lay. Anxious, for
the last of his light was wasting,
he strode the souring foreshore.
Swiftly, before the rip-tide
turned, he dug firm sand that sighed

as he lifted it. He strung his line
of a hundred hooks beyond the braid
of matted wracks by the shine
of phosphor: swifter, snood by snood,
crouching, baited. And when he stood

calf-deep to sink the anchored tag,
there were November floes of cold
incising him, shells in the under-drag
to crampon his tread. It was his way
to walk towards the morning sky

and back by water's withdrawing hem
when there were gulls enough to see by.
Sometimes, walking early, I saw him
fling into a shallow box
the flapping catch he tore from the hooks.

I lie awake, cold nights like this,
and when his memory gently shakes
the moonlight through the frosting glass
to fill my room with gulls, the sound
of him will come as a less than wind:

the barren whistle that he left
blowing across the stones and sand
to a field where the linnets lift
over him, warm as he is now, deep
in the morning of his sleep.

Lemons

I

Scented, cool and marble dark
the basilica. My unerring words
of benediction echo in the dome.
Under the banners, mumbling lips
of the brown, untouchable poor
moisten with fealty as I pass.
Great, brass double-doors swing
towards the morning, the sun
shuddering above the piazza
like a struck gong. A clangor
of hot light hovers on rinds
of faces close as a tub of lemons.
And I walk with a learned humility
under the portico, am seen,
and after a dark ovation
of rising, multitudinous birds,
clapping begins; heavy, hard, dry,
from cupped palms of practised applauders.

II

I fall awake. Acclamations
of rain are bursting; English
rain, sporadic, spontaneous,
containing silences. The room
is possessed of an after-scent
of spilt, lemon-blossom talc.
I feel the simper of my dream
about my satisfied mouth: listening
in the resonant emptiness
of an unlit, narrow stair-well
I mutter it slack. Dispassionate,
I look towards the city,
its sky awash with ceaseless neon.
Over fields planked with standing water
I see the cathedral floodlit
among houses where many lie
with many they have left, awake
without the disturbance of words.

III

Comfortably, behind my lids
I watch the recurrent boy
leave a house of cheap, flaked brick.
It is Sunday. He does not need
the lemon his mother had him smell
through the nausea of going to school:
yet he carries it, past emplacements
of guns laid up in idleness
to a camouflaged hangar
too huge for its Tiger Moth.
Up a rumbling of oil-drums
and a stack of yellow chocks
he climbs, reaches for the truss,
walks along the under-wing;
and while he recites against silence,
shrilly, into the shadowless dark
of the roof, cloudbursts of pigeons
pour out and up into the day.

IV

In a long, undreamable
gallery of unfinishing glass
in the sleep I cannot sleep,
I might stop the perfect birds
at will in the rumourless air;
listen to a subtlety of water
tapping upon lemon leaves
unmolested by any weather;
there would be warmth, latently cool
with ripening astringency:
and in that plain, unechoing hall
I should cast exactitudes of truth
with words offering homage
due to time, remembering
how a broken, boyish pontiff
lay on his actual pillow,
tired in an unbegun morning
ugly with February's drift.

PART THREE

The Night Bathers

POEMS 1966—8

(For my friends)

Nothing Besides (Neruda)

I was at one with Truth
to bring back light to the earth.

Like bread I wanted to be:
I never stopped struggling.

Here though I am with what I loved,
with the loneliness I lost;
by that rock I cannot rest.

The sea, while I am silent, works away.

Sunday Drive to the Beach

I park the car in midwinter sun.
The tailgate flashes open, then the slam
Shut slams from the sea wall. My children,
Forgetting me, lope over the marram
In comic pursuit of their salt-crazed dog.

And so starts another wholesome jag
Of ozone, an afternoon's poking
At jetsam. With empty leash I lag
Through fouled sand. A wind is thwacking
Loose flaps of felt on a summer hut,

But how bland this January, how hot
This boat is, fatigued in its oval weals
Of dead paint. I lie in my overcoat
Alongside, spent as a plank. Those oils
Flow that augur delectable sleep,

Slow under the lids – but I must keep
Awake. I stand, shake off the failed week,
And stumbling among boulders, almost trip.
But barefoot cantering the sand's wet plaque,
The children remember me, and wave,

And I wave, remembering the live
Ice of a January years ago.
I stab down the stones, into their love,
To tell them how wild swans of the starved air
Flew towards me once from the seaward snow.

Sunsets (Verlaine)

A sickly dawn
floods the fields
with a sadness drawn
from the setting sun

a sadness to sing
sweetly to my heart
that finds forgetting
in a setting sun

strange dreams these are
like suns that set
like phantoms scarlet
along some shore

merciless passing
passing merciless
like big suns setting
along some shore

Three Boys

Through steel-hawser winds of winter
Sometimes we went – but it's the slack days
Of August I remember best. We'd saunter
Hot as cork through the fishermen, to laze
In the golden ropes at the jetty head
While the sea made its soft, immeasurable lead

And the only cloud was high-gliding gulls.
I would bask, and Jim sleep, and Michael see
Invisible shoals nudging the piles
For sandhoppers. His fog-horn voice would carry
Through the heat, to tell us of the wrasse,
Dragonfly gurnet, and vast uncatchable bass

He'd seen. I'd look. Perhaps there'd be a rind
Of lemon floating like a dead anemone
Under us: but nothing else. I didn't mind
When he said I'd looked too late – not many
Months before, I'd have sworn it was true
That I'd seen those miracle fishes too.

But Big Jim minded. He stretched, long as a man,
And yawned, and told me to tell the kid to go.
When I did, he tried not to cry, and ran
Crookedly to the last of a broken row
Of lobster-pots, and out of sight. Sundown
Came, the anglers packed their tackle, and alone

Then we'd wait for the ships to use the tide.
Each vessel was a triangle of lights,
Red for the port, green for the starboard side
And white at mast-head. Some foggy nights
They vanished, leaving Jim and me no choice
But to see them plain as the fish in Michael's voice.

For John Charles Walker, Killed on Shoreham Beach

I don't think you would ever have approved
Of being in a poem. 'Mushty, look,'
I hear your spectre saying, 'keep it dark;
I wouldn't want my mates to get to know.'
But, uncle, how else can I honour you?
Time's gone when I could do the things you did.

At Cambridge I came close to what you were,
Being choked by intellectual simoom;
My most cerebral action there was the soft-
Selling of advert space in *Cambridge Left*
To the boss of a fish-and-chip saloon.
Literally, I wore the coat you wore –

The jacket of that white alpaca suit
You dared the yobs to jeer on Worthing Prom.
My pals all wondered where I'd nicked it from
And, Brando-esque in leather, named a hand
In Poker after me. Two of a kind
I think we were in the days of that coat.

On pay-days in the shipyard you played Brag
Around an oil-drum with a greasy pack
A week's wages slipped through. You'd borrow back
Enough to stand a round of beer later.
Down The Marlipins they say you were
The sort that got offered a man's last fag.

That was before the war. Sometimes your ghost
Enters my mind, dressed in some comical
Garb; aptly in white, on a bicycle,
Fresh from a battle with lime-bags; or wet
After a fifty-foot plunge for a bet
At midnight in the Adur. It was just

Your luck to get away with it. And when
I get most sick of my gentility
And all my careful life's futility –
Pruning the bloody roses for next year,
Setting the prunings tidily on fire,
Sweeping the ashes away – why, it's then

I almost envy you that booby-trap.
All alive-o you strolled to pinch firewood
From the one innocent house that still stood
On Shoreham beach. *You* never knew what it meant
To look for blood in your daily excrement;
You never knew the mine that blew you up.

Washing the Body (Rilke)

By now they were used to him. But
when the kitchen lamp was brought,

fitfully burning in a dark draught,
the Stranger was alien. His throat

the swabbed. Not knowing his past,
they lied him a life as they washed.

One of them stopped and coughed.
The heavy, vinegar sponge she left

on his face. Through the silence
the woman with her, too, had to pause.

The stiff brush let its drops tap.

Grisly, his cramped hand tried to announce
his lack of thirst throughout the house.

And did. Coughing, they resumed.
Self-consciously, more hurried,

they resumed. While, on the papered
wall, twisting, wallowing, crooked,

their shadows swam trapped in a net
till the washing was complete.

In the window, curtainless,
was brutal night. One, nameless,

lay there, clean, bare, issuing laws.

Insomniac

Walk behind night, too tired for sleep,
Through buckthorn ill of the moon.
Sea heaves in a puckered hide, thrown elephant.
Barley fields lap, and oats, awash with poppies.
Unmoor, unmoor, my arms; rehearse
Rowing to open water. Shipped oars
Would warm with salt, rough
In a sun adrift where nothing is sung.

Birth of a Merman

for Kit Barker

After the visiting waterbird had done,
Sea slid in along the final oil
And again
He knew unmillioning every cell
Of tissue under the man-skull.

All this had happened to him before,
His immemorial bodies. Once more
The soft squab
Belly was split to the fingering crab,
And bones sank slow to the ocean floor,

And it was finished, the human death.
By first morning water-light he rose
To burst in froth,
Astonishing white, spontaneous
Surf upon stillness. On the warmth

Of drifting foam rushed engender-
ing air to riffle him in the sun.
The slender
Edge of him lay for the dark when
Lightning would strike and thunder

Drop crammed power. A wave-back
Gathered into ribs, tautened the black
Weed that was skin,
Wind its knitting unguent. In
One scissoring minute he was made. Rain

Hissed awash. He felt. He was webbed.
The raw, sudden lungs accepted breath.
The grey, dabbed
Sands were astir with him. He rubbed
The weatherless corridors, searching for earth.

The Harpooning

Where the seas are open moor
and level blue, limitless,
and swells are as soft grasses
rolling over with the wind,
often to the idleness
of Azorean summer

come the great whales. Long granites
grow, slowly awash with sun,
and waves lap along black skin
like the shine of a laving
rain upon a city pavement.
Together they come, yet alone

they seem to lie. Massively
still, they bask, breathing like men.
Silent among them there is one
so huge he enters the eye
whole, leaving the rest unseen.
His sons and his cows idly

loll, as if in wait. Inside
him, too, tethered now, there waits
the bulk and strength of a herd
of a dozen rogue elephant;
they strain taut thongs of his will,
and paw against such indolence.

Anger could snap them loose –
anger, or hunger. Jungles
under a mile of ocean,
where no light has ever been,
would splinter, and the blind squid
uncoil in him like oily trees

But the squint jaws close on bone
steady as a castle door-jamb;
and, bigger than a drawbridge,
his tail flukes are calm upon
the calmer water. While the sun
still pleases him, he will grudge

himself no pleasure. He blows
old air from his old lungs, cones
rising whitely. Through the hard,
final coursings of his blood
the oars will not rouse him. Thick
blubber houses him like hot meringue.

The Pythons

Deep in caves under Java,
white snakes with purposeless eyes
live by the plain behaviour

of fanging at any noise
not of water dropped on rock.
Scuttering among runways,

they listen for where to look,
swallow, and dream a sleep of tastes;
are deaf of the want of dark

when a gatherer's lamp infests
their corridor. While poles probe
the musting, edible nests

spittled by swifts, one swung club
of light is enough to stun
lissomness stiff to a tube.

It's then the lazar-house stone
in the colourless, still pit
moves, beginning to be green

and living for being lit.
Nests stack, like clutches of skulls
in a catacomb, or split,

spilling dust the blackness pulls.
Deliberate, entranced like
a visionary, the boy fills

sacks with what he came to seek
safe within his proven cone
of brilliance; then comes back

on a swing of rope, alone.
And, knowing the white ears stare
out of glidings that begin

under his shadow once more,
he climbs to surface slowly
through deep terraces of prayer,

holding the pythons holy.

Grass

Whoever has travelled in grassless places
Remembers for ever the upward stare
Of blind earth eying out of pits
To gaze
A skull-face changeless over the bone.

I am thankful for the grass I own.
It clothes bare tilth that my
Deliberate seed refuses;
It grafts an
Unbidden skin over the permanent soil.

But I have known it fail:
Given as the snow, it is taken away
In arid summers. When evenings grow
Ungardenly
With broadcasts of oriental war,

I have stood at my open door
Remembering the wild rice of Asia
Teeming in waste, unpeopled swamps,
And the blanched
Lepers corroding through the cities.

Near them, where no grass is,
The slat-flanked cattle sometimes come,
Bringing a shrivelled cud gathered
From far off.
Rare seed falls on them from long-flighted birds.

Moon Ashes

For longer than time is left me,
Breast-high among the ashes I swam.
While there was earth-light to travel by,
I knew behind their white, soft,
Terrible collapse upon themselves
And how they evened over where I had come
Like windless waters levelling after a skiff.

The dark came, easier. I guess
What silent myriads will fall
Upward from my path, beginnings of snow,
As though this were Earth. Fierce
For hard, high ground where no fleck settles,
I shoulder away from the crater's centre,
Carrying no flag, no token crucifix.

Snow Asthma

Sifting into silence
    Until the yard was filled,
Snow was a sudden comer
    When I was a child.

Bullfinches were in bloom
    On a bough of dead apple;
As though the moon made daylight,
    Shadow was purple.

Seldom as bereavement
    Came snow. For a brief
Morning my mother's face
    Looked underlit with grief.

She threw ashes on the path
    And dug out the gate;
She kept watch along the road
    Until it grew late.

Whatever was to come
    That time kept away,
But through my window's wide-awake
    And sunken eye

I stared from my smother
    While unmolestable snow
Thick on a conifer-top
    Stifled its crow.

Thaw

A cooling sudden
as snowfall by night
made love's earth harden;

with crystals of hate
winter had trodden
our solitude tight.

Then we were broken
for once in a way;
we were turned to the sun

and our frost was taken
like double-dug clay
whose shives fall open.

Journey Back

Uncertain day in certain
winter. The Midland counties
clodded in November's ruck.
At mid-morning's latent dark,
air the violet of rubbed eyes,
it looks too late to begin

back. After a dozen miles
of wharf, slate roof on the sag,
I glimpse a gruel of hills
past railed Victorian schools, black
terrace-ends, metallic slag,
and feast on a broken oak

harbouring crows. Looping wires
lead, full of silent voices,
home, southward out. If I spoke
to my family now, heard noises
of their playing, like fires
crackling live in the kiosk,

I'd warm no more than the least
acre of this loneliness;
vastly its landscape swims, lost
beyond its minor byroads –
land without finish. I press
on, making my diamonds

in the tilth of the year's first
snow. Headlamps winnow its chaff;
the windscreen packs with mooncrust.
London, Surrey and the Weald
hush under me. Close enough
now to a recognized cold –

this line of poplars I know,
branches cordoned like police –
guiltily I stop with less
than ten easy miles to go
and dial my number. My voice
seems confident as it says,

It's good to be coming home,
look forward to seeing you,
having a practised cadence,
habitual, therefore true.
And as the last turnings come
through the hanger wood, I sense

a relief in familiar
landscapes of a solitude
rooted here: that will be known
season and season beyond
this night, this cold, these thrown
regattas of foundered snow.

A Place of Trees

for Bernard Price

They've been felling. From the copse
Beside the lane, all day long,
I have listened to the collapse
Of timber, the mad saw wailing

Agonized while it spun free,
And then the blade's grateful moan
As it cracked another tree
Like a dog splintering a bone.

Thinking I'd take a last look,
I came when the men had left.
In the failing light the smoke
Of their bonfires lingered soft

Among the wilting laurels
That used to grow in the dark.
The raw stumps were tar-barrels
Open to the shooting spark,

But by those flares I could recall
No individual trunk,
No limb, or any single
Leaf of what lived here. I think

In this winter night only
Of close, high-summer shadows
Gathering over a lonely
Visitor. A dirt path shows

The way he came to this place
Of trees. It leads into a dry
Field, and fields beyond, then space
Beyond the last star of the sky.

Hothouse

There was a place in his mind
where the man could be alone
from choice, free from his children
and not at home to his friend;
where husband was husbandman

not to be called to his food
but in his own time. He made
all weather that entered; took
rain from a pipe at the flood
or trickle, as the mood took

him. He could put out the sun
with lime-wash over the glass,
could waft on his leaves cool airs
at will. He saw a season
breed that was not the summer's,

all summer. He was a god
come to crucify his trees
on wires. Whatever would grow
would grow as he thought was good.
In winter he lit his fires

covertly in a furnace-house:
new stars to warm his planet.
Lamps left to burn through midnight
lit the sliding snow-waters
from the roof. He would delight

in visiting his blossom,
come spring, with a rabbit's scut.
Before the first bees were out,
busily his hands would swarm;
infallible crops would set.

When he bruised the ripened fruit,
he savoured an urgent juice
that spilled in his hand. The house
had swollen more than he could eat.
Nectarines were everyone's.

In an hour they'd pick him bare
and leave goodbyes. He would stay
a little while, after. He
would be tired at the door
where the strange day-lilies sway.

Hillpath

Soft for the sun
as no stone
for footfall deaf

hot chalk I
trod through the
moth noon led

to thick sprucewood
floors listening
for conefall

Stone

Too tired, after, even to close my eyes,
In the half-dark I saw her skin for stone,
So motionless. I waited for the rise
Or falling of her breast, but there came none:
She seemed too tired, after, even to breathe,

And does not feel these lizard fingers writhe
Over her now. I'll let my lids half close
And bask till the last of her warmth has gone
And the morning's entering cloudlight shows
Her stone for flesh, my flesh for stone again.

Dewdrop

Blue in a lupin-leaf
after-dawn diamond
unliquidly
shone

A simple brilliant
eating the face
of the morning
sun

A crystal of night as
hard as star-glint
fixed as owl-
eye

Closing upon some inner
darkness tinily
it mirrored
me

Swallows

A day of winter-slaked April.
Bobbers on a wire at a wall –
trindles of fire-blued iron
that any wind twitches – twirl
and are lifted into swallows.

Little particles of thirst,
the red of summer brickdust
are those throats among a month
avaricious of its damp; fust
of the whitening lichen,

buffed by delicate bellies,
comes live out of its ice.
Blue is warm of swallows' wings:
rich spillings of their sapphires
glint along the dark, nettled end

of garden. They are my claim –
over half a world they come,
crop-full of Africa, to lodge
in crevices of my home.
In honorance of such plenty,

I make them a plot of hotness
to skim upon: hibiscus,
hyssop, pools of buddleia,
a humming of mulberries.
I fork the brown mulch of one

summer less into my earth
as warm weather falls. Nothing can encourage their coming
again. I leave them be, with
an untouched, vulnerable clutch

of another year's small flesh.
Soon my eyes must relinquish
them. When the hips are redder
than the roses were, they'll brush
my willow a final time,

flying out of the house.
And, a continent deep, I sense
some other self – between us,
paltry, diminishing oceans
and arid, vanishing land.

Kraaled in a vast and untreed
veld, his sleep is troubled.
My wall of lichen relapses white.
In the night he lifts his head,
listening for ultimate swallows.

The Sleep of Apples (Lorca)

I long to sleep the sleep of apples, far
from the blast of graveyards,
sleep the sleep of the boy who tried
to cut his heart out over the sea.

Tell me no more the dead can't bleed,
that the rotted mouth still asks for water.
The atrocities of grass,
the snake-jawed moon
that chews before dawn –
no concern of mine.

A little while I want
to sleep, a little while, a
minute, a century.
But let
everybody know: I have not died;
the golden stable is at my lips,
I am the west wind's crony,
I, the vastest shadow of my teardrops.

Come daybreak, pull the sheet over me
from the dawn's flung fistful of ants;
use hard water to wet my shoes,
to make the first light's scorpion-pincers slip.

For I long for the sleep of apples, and
to learn some song to purge me of earth;
long to be beside the solemn child
who tried to cut his heart out over the sea.

Elderberries

Every night I would pass the elderberries
Severally aglimmer from a composite eye
Sunk in the dark of leaves that desolately
Stank to the village lamplight. Memories

Of elders past I gathered, those within reach,
Picking at will. Almost, I could almost touch
The thick inflorescences of autumn stars
That colder air remembered of the elders,

So soon after summer. Skies brimmed a taut pool
Of known patterning. I searched for the blossom
To drop from some forgotten tree, but random
Petals drowned evanescently. Beyond recall,

Whatever it was that had been terrible,
Once. Elders, elders: I had by heart the smell,
And it had to do with loneliness – often,
Hot from the stare of an unfrequented lane,

I'd snatched off a hollow stem to dig my nail
Hard and deep into the white, the secret pith.
But it wasn't this. Something else I had with
Me, out in the empty street. I'd pass my wall

Encrusted with pygmy, indigo mirrors
Night after night, wondering: step out of doors
Straight into them, into the berries, and slide
Fast from the lamplight edging their unlit side.

The Night Bathers

I walk, a stranger here,
in alien, emptying Wales
through orange montbretia
wild among fallen walls
of a left, profitless farm
where only visitors come.

Along the promontory
warm of an indolent lick
Of August water, hazes
close on a momentary crow.
Dark is a lenient harm
over Cardiganshire.

I am alone as now
my son is alone. Below
the headland he worries at sleep
where bushes breathe the evening
in. Troubles of honeysuckle
film his air. Remorse of mine

wrapped him about too warm;
he wrestled off my comforting.
A thunder sensed in other hills
has moved away. Rain would ease him
but it will not rain. All day,
as sands of little birds lifted

in a strapping summer wind
that smacked canvas brittle with sun,
I was aware of health and
used it bitterly in play,
pitiless against the man
growing from the sullen boy

rid of me now. I made him
run out the slack of the tide
till sand was dry on his tiredness
and the sea was a far, shut bud.
Now, as he ebbs in a dream
from the pull of my contrition,

I hear the night bathers come
over the yelping stones. I see
by astonishing bonfires
in an idleness of yachts
my father running down the beach
twenty grown years ago, at home;

when he was young to understand
why, momently out of the night
and purposeful beyond the reach
of all his worry, I had swum
deep into banks of sea-fret
too far to have to answer him.

Bonfire

Final nightfall of summer.
I scrape a match at the wall,
cup safe the flame. Cracked hands smell
of earth and ripening pear
that I breathe, beginning fire.

All afternoon was the waft
from blue fields, the stubble-scorch,
pricking me to this. I crouch
like an ancient to my craft,
knowing this moment to lift

dry leafage to little twigs
and lean to a locked apex
the slats of a smashed apple-box.
Gripping broken ladder-legs,
the blaze skips up to long logs

of old, wasp-ruddled fruitwood.
I rub with a rough stick spark-
showers down, petals from the bark,
and listen for the first, hard
apricot fireball to thud

dull among the underheat.
And it is done, my pleasure.
I smother the sprinting fire
with swaths of nettles I swapped
an hour since, failed dahlias ripped

from faded ceremony,
and pulped, unflowered irises.
I watch as the smoke rises,
inclining slow towards my
house, and upwards, and away,

then leave my fire in darkness.
Indoors, with every window
tight, I start to feel the glow
of nettle-throb on my face,
and sit with smoke's bitterness

steeped in my clothes. My closed eyes
remember a settling gleed,
white, red, clinking. Outside,
where the last of summer burns,
my soil lies clean for the ice.

Mary's Carol (Lope de Vega)

Holy angels in the palms,
hold your branches still
while my baby is asleep;

O palm trees of Bethlehem
tossed in the angry winds,
make no sound for Him

while my baby is asleep,
but hold your branches still.
God's little boy is tired

with weeping – let Him rest
from His mild tears now;
hold your branches still

while my baby is asleep.
The rock frosts about Him
and He has no coverlet;

holy angels of the trees,
hold your branches still
so my little child may sleep.

Joseph Speaks to the Midwife of Bethlehem

You made me wait outside the stable door.
You had your work to do. Nobody knew
It was the Son of God my Mary bore.

In Bethlehem the winter nights are raw;
But while the wind from Hebron's summit blew,
You made me wait outside. The stable door

Was sealed with frost. I made a fire and saw
The cattle restless when the cinders flew.
It was the Son of God my Mary bore

That night, beside the manger, on the floor,
Frightened and cold. Little though I could do,
You made me wait. Outside the stable door

You called to me, told me to gather straw
For Him to lie upon. A baby Jew
It was – the Son of God my Mary bore

Had looks like mine. And in His face I saw
This light that I forgive you by: for though
You made me wait outside the stable door,
It *was* the Son of God my Mary bore.

February Poem

The hours of daylight must be lengthening now:
I walked among the frost and noticed how
The last, softening snowdrops were in thaw;
Then, stepping between flecks of shadow, saw
The first collapse of crocuses begun,
Yellowy in small fritterings of sun.
Ridiculous with delight, I hurried home.

But I stare from a winter-facing room
To think how premature the petal-fall
Of laurustinus by the churchyard wall;
And as the minutes edge me from the light
Into this perceptibly shorter night,
I sense a northerly gathering of air
Prising another bud of my despair.

PART FOUR

Gloves to the Hangman

POEMS 1969—72

(For my brother)

A Celebration for Autumn

Once more I welcome a purer darkness
Of evening in the hour of the year
Between summer and an end of summer,
When the soft air is songless as moss
Over the barn where the swallows are

Restless. Something has wearied the sun
To yellow the unmolested dust
On the bitter quince; something is lost
From its light, letting waxen bees drown
In their liquor of fatigue. But by last

Shadows of another season gone,
I live into beginning autumn
To see its silver, broken column
Of thready smoke ascending. Someone
Has gathered up his few leaves fallen

On the morning's webby lawn, who knows
Nothing of how I share them. I think
Of his hands at the live fire, and thank
Him in his private wood for what grows
Commonly for us toward the stars

I recognize of winter to come.
And I remember an August once,
With armfuls of slushing leaves, left since
Noon to dry by the hedge they fell from,
Shiny as the shears. Could we burn them

Now, I wheedled my grandfather, now?
Everything in its own due time,
He said, for fires need cold and autumn
Dark if you want their flowers to grow;
And who was I to call down the snow

Before its proper season? The weeks
Frittered on beyond the old man's dying,
And the ready pears, and my crying
In his garden-rows of empty sticks.
His fire shot higher than hollyhocks

One night when the smell of dead summer
Was too much to bear. It was for me,
Who had had hardly a breath easy
From the heavy hammer of asthma,
That frost assembled in that glimmer

Of thrown smoke, and prized into my blood
Like the feel of knives over the skin.
I lived on, into its cold. Again
I tread through a crisping grass; the hard
Air closes again, and I am glad.

Some troubled sleep it may take to bear
The slump of one less summer – but clean
The sun tomorrow, or the frail rain.
I shall breathe in refreshed September.
I have much to thank my autumns for.

One Magpie for Sorrow

Now the rafters lift and shake
On blunt struts above the loft
And the flues whine down from the dark.
November again, month of my birth,
Blanches the stones bare to the earth

And gusts a single magpie, bereft
And cowering, to the stripped magnolia.
In my hearth the cold cinders shift
As I stare from the place where I belong.
Riffling another dying year, among

Dumb tokens of all I choose to be,
I pretend nothing can change. Yet,
As the day fades over the broken country
And this old white house prey to the weather,
I know my lie; know too well what other

Selves might enter. The magpie that
Cannot be hidden by darkness or by snow
Crouches under the wind. I shut out
Winter, whatever must come to pass.
Brittle twigs grint against the glass.

Snow in Southern England

Not rare, or common, the snow
that visits our winters here:
a thin inch for every year
perhaps, and a foot or so
lost from the north one year in four;

and sometimes a stifled door
pushes back on a path of dead
sparrows grey as bits of bread,
broken to the dark before
some white moor fallen from the night.

But we live in a temperate
place, and never know true cold.
Brittling bones can grow old
in us, unsplintered by ice. Not
harder than my cruel summer doves

is the flocculence that lives
its day on the barren damson tree.
Warmed over by this January
sun, tomorrow the blush roofs
will show another season gone

of snow. I'd wish no more, more often,
than the falls we have, frequent as
sorrow. Or, brief as happiness,
want less, less often. The moon
risen this night is a white crow

roosting in a blizzard of stars.
The wind is stilled, and all I know
that I'd desire would be eyes
for dark beyond our buried places,
further off than this illumined snow.

New Forest Ponies

They stopped from a gallop. Steam
left them like epiphanies
loose in the dusk. I saw them
whisking at snowflakes like flies.

It was a pair of forest
mares, briskets slung like hammocks
of fat matelots. With rapt lust
they browsed remnants of picnics

beside the Brockenhurst road.
Hobos, they rifled litter-bins,
turfing out chicken bones; then stood
casually among beer-cans,

posed for a snapshot album.
I nudged them along the verge
until their stallion came
prancing a disremembered rage

through the ice twilight. His strength
was flagged, a softening thong
of wash-leather. The cushy south
where he lives, where I belong,

would paddock him for gymkhanas,
currying his fourteen hands
to a genteel handsomeness.
Now he smelt like failing ponds,

shut cinemas. He began to come
at me. Gripping the fence-post,
I waited. But he ambled, a tame
elderly man in tweeds, lost

in some reverie of war,
all wildness shrunk. White of eyes
was mush, the shown teeth sulphur
dull. He let me feel him – thews,

veins, worn cordage to the touch.
I held him grass on my palm.
He cadged himself a sandwich;
mooched away, slavering jam.

Letter to Barbados

Dear far-off brother, Thank you for yours,
And for the gift you send of little shells.
Evening. It has been an April day
Like any you remember. I guess
How you miss the English spring, the way
A shower-cloud over a hillside spills

Between sunlight and sunlight, slowly.
Is it half a year since you've been gone?
While you gather up windfall nutmegs,
My white magnolia flowers fly
Withering from the twig like cotton rags
I must rake tomorrow from the lawn.

I wonder what news you want to hear:
That everything remains as it was
Before you left? That we are well? That
Swallows, like molecules of summer,
Warm on the wall behind the dovecote?
All is satisfactory in this house.

I read over again what you tell me.
Outside your window you've had grapefruits
Ripening through winter; there's a calf
You love to let suck your fingers. I
Relish these images of your new life,
Though the dinning sun above you hurts

My eyes as I gaze. Easier for you,
Perhaps, to think back to the shadow
Of this temperate, darkening garden,
Where I sit and look for my last few
Doves to come home. They will soon swoop down,
Just as you recall they always do,

From the roof; each full throat soon will soothe
Nightfall once more. This morning I made
A first cut of the grass since autumn.
It smelt sweet in the sun, in the swathe
Where I left it to dry. I fetched my gun
And sought out a sickly dove and killed

It clean, and let it warm where it fell.
Whether it is white, loosened feathers
I glimpse in the half-dusk or blossoms
Lifting with the wind I cannot tell,
But I am glad to have you share them.
There are words not used between brothers,

And you will understand if I send
No more than these, the shrivelling details
Of another lost and uneventful day.
The birds are folded now. I shall stand
A moment more in the dead grass we
Walked on. My palms close cold over shells.

The Émigrés

Visiting from Britain, I take my ease
In a Massachusetts yard. Willows
Have opened overnight along the ridge;
This is the second spring I've seen this year.

I watch as my once-English hostess
Moves across the shadow of the spruces
At her door. She calls her home a cottage
And puts on homeliness like a sweater.

She's tried, over and over, to grow grass
Around the place; grass, and a few roses,
And even, look, a bit of privet hedge
To remind her of home in Warwickshire.

She brings me bourbon in an ice-packed glass
And tinkles on about the neighbours' houses.
Americanisms glint like a badge
Pinned onto her. She much prefers life here,

She protests, remembering what life was
For her in England – the dirt, rising prices,
Always having to live at the edge
Of her nerves. Not to mention the weather.

I stir my drink. 'I'd not mind it either,
For a while,' I say. Martins lodge,
Like my swallows at home, in crevices
Of her roof. 'Oh, purple martins, those

Damn things. I'll have to rake them down from there,'
She says. 'Mind you, it's not that I begrudge
Them somewhere to live. But if you saw the mess
They make, you wouldn't think me heartless.'

Now, in his office near a fall-out shelter
High over downtown Boston, husband Reg
Will be turning his calendar (English Views
In Summertime) into May. The two of us,

Last evening, swept the last of the winter
Cones into a heap. Outside his garage
Afterwards, he told me, watching the flames,
Of all his new, perpetual worries:

There's his job – they daren't have kids. And Russia.
And how he'll never keep up with the mortgage.
Not to mention the droughts, the six-foot snows,
In the yard where nothing English ever grows.

La Más Bella Niña (Góngora)

The loveliest girl
of our home town,
the bride of a day,
is widowed and alone;
for the light of her eyes
to the war has gone,
and she tells her mother
who hears her mourn:

O leave me, leave me
to weep by the sea.

You told me, mother,
when I was young,
how pleasure is brief
but suffering long,
and, yes, you warned me
of him gone today,
who has taken the key
of my freedom away,

O leave me, leave me
to weep by the sea.

May these eyes that once
could see with delight
serve only for tears
and not for sweet sight;
they no longer have
a more fitting use,
for he's gone to the war
who was my peace.

O leave me, leave me
to weep by the sea.

Do not restrain me
or seek to find fault;
I deserve your lashes,
but don't rub salt.
If you wish me well,
don't treat me ill;
I'd be better off dead,
and silent, and still.

O leave me, leave me
to weep by the sea.

O my sweet mother,
who would not groan
though in her breast
beats a heart like stone;
who would not weep
as the years pass by
and the leaves of her youth
all wither and die?

O leave me, leave me
to weep by the sea.

The nights slip by
and the eyes have gone
that kept these lids
wide open till dawn;
gone; may they never
from loneliness stare
as mine from this bed
that has room to spare.

O leave me, leave me
to weep by the sea.

Polecats in Breconshire

Fine moths dropped from the darkness,
drifted the fallings of swarf
to dust the grasses whitely
where whitely flew the first scarf
of an owl as quiet as wool.

It was time for them to come
hot from a clammy chamber
under the summer mountain,
test the close air, and clamber
the foul chippings at their door.

They stood, rare as royalty,
in black and purplish fur
matted with the sweat of sleep;
relaxed as flaccid rubber,
they were ready to be stretched

the length of night's territory.
Seldom glimpsed by a human –
except, perhaps, at evening
by lonely widow-women
musty as old whinberries –

they loped for no enemy
they knew. Over the bracken
they leaped free; among the few,
too few to count, five of them ran
their bodies smooth in the dew.

And all the while there was night
they would shark through the thickets,
incising behind the skull
beasts that would be the pellets
of their pleasure. Armoured with

stench, and teeth to score tungsten,
they would slummock on fat eels.
On some road the good mother
would suckle her whelps. I would wonder
what they were, under my wheels.

Afterwards

Afterwards, we quarrel from love
And once again we are back
In our disparate bodies.
The room cools, almost darkness,

My fingers gripping the fallen quilt.
You lie as if at the edge of the sea,
The sun gone off the water.
Hair has the slipperiness of eelgrass.

Oh, the words you flung, I hear them,
Pebbles tumbling, smoothened with use;
But hurting; but individual; belonging
To us – worth keeping for themselves.

While you sleep, I gather them.
You shift. I listen for the city.
Tyre-hiss, a draining breakwater;
I remember finding a kittiwake, dead.

You are so cold. I should cover
This illicit skin awash in the moon.
I lift you as though you were mine
To keep. Let me see your eyes.

Villanelle

I would wish to die in some other place
Than where visitors come. I would be thrown
One morning of the winter on my face

In porous earth that would not leave the trace
Of where I lie. Not that I want it known
I would wish to die. In some other place,

Some other time, I might argue that case:
Waking, say, to a cancer and alone
One morning. Of the winter, on my face

I feel a flint wind blow, though clouds chase
May shadows. I dream the chalk hill whose bone
I would wish to die in. Some other place

Might serve as well for earth's final embrace;
And small matter where, so long as no one,
One morning of the winter, on my face

Touch the skull smile the soft rain will erase.
The morning finds my flesh as warm as stone.
I would wish to die in some other place.
One morning of the winter. On my face.

Boy By a River

Lymph, bled from a dead chalk,
and gauzes of watered milk
slubbered a certain turf
among dry hills, far off,
and lived, kindling his river.

But he was young – such inklings never
trickled into his bigger knowledge.
He brazened the estuary's edge
by a rusty wharf, and could stare
only to seaward. For there

where he lived it was a wide
sliding on the silent tide;
or, shrunk to its thews, sawed itself raw
across broken rock and the bare
ribs of picked ships. And all he knew

of meadow brooks that grew
pure between upland pasture –
of barley fields upriver
that spared through their flints thin
tributaries of cress hidden

from fish – he had learned from a friend
the fresh waters had lately drowned,
who had spoken of simple shallows
where the swimming was good. Those
reaches would flow through his mind

always; already their pools wound
a body round in an endless whirl
for his memory. In time, he would while
a summer's hour tracing the source,
and with his man's strong hand force

back for an instant the feeble
killer into dumb earth. It would dribble
in his tight fingers slowly,
then he would dry them. Now he let fly
his stones that the brimming ebb

accepted with a sip. In the crab
holes he supposed they would rest,
too deep, too heavy to move. The last
of the white and rolling bones might be
shifting somewhere near. This he

believed, though for years he'd refuse
all else he was told of the river. His
eyes fixed on the cormorant he knew,
he would be old before the blue
jewel of a kingfisher filled them

and he followed with the wind upstream
that lifted ripples into the flood.
There were lost otter runs, his friend had said,
and long golden mullet that laze
under the banks where wildfowl graze.

After Drought

The river was its dregs –
Not water but stuck dags
Flung from the sun. One pool
Shrank to a cellar smell.

You could have picked trout
Like flowers. They had got
Wedged in lilies, each back
Stretched and dry as a stalk.

In the night I remembered
Them pressed tight to the lid
Of their element as
I grappled my jammed windows.

I had fire-damp on the lung.
The thought of gills pummelling
As brute gas had me sweat.
When first it thundered it

Fluttered like a failing
Heart. Puny lightning
Flared brief as match struck
In a gust. Fragments broke

From the brick air – bits
Of wind and stabbed, long spots
To the spread palm. I came
Outside toward the storm

And stand now bare to its axe.
It smashes black to the trunks
Of great trees. While I breathe
Deep from seething rain, wraith

Shadows fan across grass
Whiter than gravel. Rivers
Are rising to their reeds.
A poem swims from its words.

August

It was a slow
river that slid
wide through level
country of fen
and of soft-earth
celery fields,

making no sound
of water all
one afternoon
but flowing dark
as leafage swept
in a wet heap,

no wind to make
its rushes creak,
stem against stem,
or rain to fall
hissing on its
taut water-skin.

It was gallons
calm as a vat
someone has stirred
and left to work
in its own time
to clarify.

It licked itself
as quietly as
a cat its fur
and no skiff came
or wherry on
the turning curds.

And but for the
flying dabchick
that sheered from my
quietness I
might not have moved
my eyes away

from the river's
porcelain surface
something must smash,
or ever known
how near the sea
downstream would flash

for a moment
as the last sun
of August died
in a closing
gap of summer
mist, autumn mist.

Pig Pig

In 1386, the tribunal of Falaise sentenced a sow to be mangled and maimed in the head and forelegs, and then to be hanged, for having torn the face and arms of a child and thus caused its death . . . As if to make the travesty of justice complete, the sow was dressed in man's clothes and executed on the public square near the city-hall at an expense to the state of ten sous and ten deniers, besides a pair of gloves to the hangman.

(E.P. Evans: *The Criminal Prosecution & Capital Punishment of Animals)*

I

Hefty, she was, that beast.
Sunned herself in the crust
of cruds she had lain in.
She was blacker than sin.

She dabbled her great crotch
in swill. If you would scratch,
her with a bit of stick
you'd picked out of the muck,

she would grin like a slut.
She slobbered on the gate
her wench's gratitude
for apples. She was lewd

for putrid meat; crunched rough
splinters from a slate trough;
had a go at iron. She
was a whore, couldn't be

satisfied. We served her
with an old, borrowed boar.
He had to be dragged back
like hot dung on a truck.

II

Pigs are things. In Falaise
we esteem our horses.
Being proud, noble men
we prefer to be known

for our stables, not for
sour sties we would rather
hide from the off-comer.
In that stinking summer

I left a lass to feed
my swine. I had to ride
to the fair with a string
of thoroughbreds. Yearling

colts I'm famous for – ask
any man if I'd risk
a good reputation
palming off a dud 'un.

Prices fetched high that year.
Due to some foreign war
even your knock-kneed geld-
ing weighed his worth in gold.

III

I sold, had a skinful
of the best brewer's ale,
then headed out of town
astride my stallion.

One of the lads it was
found me in the bushes.
He'd come from mucking-out
and, by God, he smelt it.

But he hadn't the reek
of horse-dung. On his cheek
was a filthy sow-smear,
wet with a big soft tear.

I got up and whipped him
for saying I should come
back quick. He found my purse
and whistled in my horse.

Again I larruped him,
the lout. Then he said something about his sister,
dead. I dawdled faster.

IV

The brat was on a board,
her bits. The sow had gnawed
her face from her ringlets.
I'd seen sows break piglets –

runts of their abundance –
and swallow them. What chance
could a soft-boned child have
with jaws a man can't move

once they clamp? Someone had
bound the stump arms with bed-
linen ripped into strips.
The feet, gaunt as stirrups,

were bare, the batwing skin
left untorn. I drank down
a stoup of cider while
they simmered camomile

to make the corpse smell sweet.
She'd not an ounce of fat
on her. I saw quite plain
something had to be done.

V

Not that it was my fault,
mind. Peasants worth their salt
know better than allow
kids inside with a sow.

When she'd done bawling I
fetched the mother to my
house. She stank in her rags,
that hag treading my rugs.

She meant bother. She could
not stop the stable-lad
from gabbing in the pub,
she said. I let her sob

when I offered money,
felt tender for her. She
had, after all, been a nice
bit of *jus primae noctis*.

I'd see to it, I said.
She clawed her tangled head.
I couldn't see how, yet
I said I'd see to it.

VI

In her sty sprawled my sow-
murderess. I heard low
grunts as she permitted
suck. In the sun she bled

gently from a bludgeon-
gash. She'd been given one
hard across her poor old neck
with a blunted mattock.

Her litter swarmed on her
like lice on a scalp. Where
blood was she let them lick.
A pair of nipples stuck

out spare, like pinnacles.
Stout iron manacles
bit deep in her trotters.
Troubled by flies she was.

She lay helpless as scum
in a dungeon. They'd come
and chained their prisoner.
I felt angry for her.

VII

Ugly-mouthed and quiet
the men-folk stood about,
grim with clubs. I saw they
wished an eye for an eye.

Moment upon moment
they stood about, silent.
Their dumbness spoke of death,
of a tooth for a tooth.

With meekness they behaved.
Not a one would have dared
to murmur a word or
walk to the pigsty door.

The sow moaned from her pain
like a cancered woman.
I told them to go home.
I'd see them right, I told them.

Sunlight slammed on the dung
between us. The men hung
bare heads. Their cowardice
fattened on my promise.

VIII

When they buried the kid,
I processed at the head
of the cortège. If I'd
not been at that graveside,

things might have turned bad. My
tribute was a lily-
wreath, the biggest of all.
The mother seemed grateful.

It was I let the box
nice and slow to the six-
foot hole, was I let drop
a clod onto the cheap

wood lid. Then it was I
that led them solemnly
by the chain of their grief
to my welcoming roof.

I that threw wide the door.
I that spoke of the Law.
I that called upon God
to exact blood for blood.

IX

I found a precedent:
a bullock had been sent
mangled to the scaffold
for murdering a child.

Unravelling the Latin,
I knew it could be done:
the family would attest
and I'd see to the rest.

I hired the village thug
to guard the convict pig
He fed her bread, not swill.
The parish got the bill.

I called in Maître Jehan,
my boozing companion,
to prosecute. Some sense-
less lush got the defence.

We booked the city hall
for the day of the trial.
Judge Rouge, swigging my wine,
appointed me hangman.

X

With all due reverence
the oafs gave evidence
on the day. In the dock
my sow slithered in muck.

Once she managed to drag
her bulk up like a lag
and lean over. Laugh!
It was farce, right enough.

But we played it serious:
only let po-faces
slacken for Rouge's jokes.
We wanted no mistakes

at this stage of the game.
The court-room was a slum
of roughs turning ugly
looks on the likes of me.

Jehan pitched it good and strong
though, and nothing went wrong.
The sow was found guilty
of eating flesh on a Friday.

XI

Mangle and hang the sow,
old Rouge said: Do it now.
I was aproned, masked and gloved.
That was the bit I loved.

God, it was Hell's delight.
I got that chained-up brute
again and again in
the limbs. Cracking the spine

was like splitting a flint
with a grubber. I bent
a great crowbar on her,
smashing her to rubber,

let the wet brain slop out
like spawn in a bucket.
Slut, I was thinking, slut,
by Christ don't you love it.

What really pricked me on
was having that whoreson
rabble agog as I
did that thing in a sty.

XII

After I'd had enough,
somehow they prized me off
her cadaver. They dressed
it up, at my request,

in clothes I provided:
shirt and breeches of red
velveteen, my best grey
bonnet of soft corduroy.

They sat it on a cart
with me up beside it.
Garlanded, we were hauled
in style to the scaffold.

We had to take a winch
to that heap of a wench;
with ropes round her armpits
we raised her hundredweights.

She dripped like a vast bag
of fruit on a licking dog.
The mob cheered. I could see
they pretended she was me.

XIII

The carcass (hangman's perks)
was mine. I cut some hunks
of offal for the kites,
butchered the rest as joints

for salting down. I ate
well all that winter. It
had been a good day's work
when that sow became pork.

We had some fun. I got
some good gloves out of it.
It was the parish paid
the profits my cronies made.

Even the peasants did
well – one less mouth to feed.
And my fame got around.
In all France you'll not find

a richer ranch than mine.
I can die a happy man,
knowing how justice was seen
through me to have been done.

Letter to Marcel Proust

I

Monsieur, when I first met you (introduced
by a Cambridge don eighteen years ago)
there wasn't much about you I cared for.
Semites I loathed, and next to Semites, queers;
never having fancied fellers, I fought off
two-pound notes with roustabout righteousness,
and duffed up a bent yid once with a wire brush.
What's more, my father being a working bloke
who'd been on the dole through my 'thirties boyhood,
I'd learned by heart to put grub before ethics,
so that the world of Albertine and Madame Verdurin
unfolding between your punctilious semi-colons
wasn't, so to speak, du côté de chez moi.
To one of my generation of yobbos
who had inherited the posher universities,
all that palaver in scented drawing-rooms
was dated as Zeppelins, a right load of shite.
We turned every snobbery upside-down
and parodied a life we never would live:
(not for us the tea-time punt to Grantchester
but sooner a canoe to a pub in Trumpington).
But, Thanks, mate, I told my broken supervisor,
bidding him tara with a wave of the ration-book
that marked the page we'd got to in *Swann*.
One day you'll remember all this, he said,
moithering off towards the Combination Room,
à la recherche du ton perdu.

II

Today, bombing southwards on Autoroute 6
à mi-chemin between Paris and Lyon,
one of my bus-load of dumb Yankee students
offered me a madeleine from a plastic bag.
Ever the pedagogue, I seized the opportunity
to give my spiel (lasting 40 kilometres)
on the involuntary memory, monsieur, and you.

Christ, what a drag – like, man, who needs it?
was what I got from the weirdo freak.
(Though later, at the zinc in the comfort-station
I smiled to observe that the woolly number
was dunkin' a thoughtful Donut in a demi-tasse.)
Oh, the immutable ghastliness of students!
Marcel (est-il permis?), I too am nostalgic
for the decencies of life I see in decay:
I want no part of the acid-head commune
sharing out equally its bread and its crabs
(any more than I'd want the return of privilege
and the tittling *Tatler* and its snaps of debs);
yet maybe we're wrong to despair of the future,
its perspective of instant beds stretching end to end.
There will always be those to share our snobbery
for what comes difficult, like Art and Love,
and even (dare one mention it?) tolerance
by which, since Israel and the Wolfenden Report,
hetero queer-bashing fascists like me
have learned, with time, to be friends with such as you.

Sundays (Laforgue)

How aimless, passionless, the rain is, lover,
Raining endlessly into the river . . .

The river sleeps in its Sunday serge;
Upstream, downstream, not one barge.

Evensong is pealing over the town,
Along the riverbank no couples are seen.

A girls' school passes (poor little loves!)
Several already with winter gloves.

Here's one with neither gloves nor coat,
Dressed all in grey, a sorry sight.

She's broken ranks – she's a fair runner!
But O, my God, what *has* got into her?

Head-first she's flinging herself into the water,
No boatman or Alsatian to get her.

The lights go on; how late it's getting:
Think of the town, its cosy setting.

The rain keeps raining, dampening the river,
Aimlessly, with no passion whatsoever.

PART FIVE

Burning the Ivy

POEMS 1973—7

(For Margaret)

Moving

Do not attempt to sleep – your strangeness
Arouses the new house. Amazed floors,
Unaccustomed yet to what is yours,
Shift to the burden of what you bring;
Overhead, the loft that encloses

A fresh store of sentimental junk
Creaks from your broken bits of childhood.
Sometimes maybe it's all to the good
To touch, to rearrange all you own
Elsewhere. But in someone else's sink,

Though it's yours now and paid for, even
A cup can remind you of who you are,
And what you were, and why you are here.
From choice, or by accident, or both,
Once more you've humped your stuff. The oven

Was worst, its squat, impervious bulk
Grudging each inch. Yet plain heaviness,
Lifted and lifted, doesn't oppress
Like those gross abstracts we can't dispose
Of. They arrive with the morning milk.

Christmas Apples

Year-long, weekdays, I pass an orchard.
Mornings, where its windbreak poplars are,
The engine warms and I change into top
Toward the day. There's nothing to see
Of fruit-trees from the road. Blossom-time,

A dry thaw of blown petals may sift
To the ditch, soon gone; and winter nights,
When I slow for the corner near home,
Sometimes I picture the stiff ballet
Of trees imploring frost from starlight:

But, back in the warmth, forget them. Once
A year – a Sunday in December –
I drive to a warehouse at the heart
Of an acreage seeming vaster than
Memory tends. Black banners, crows flutter

High over the fields. I park the car
In an empty lot, walk to the edge
Of the same, leafless plantation where,
A twelvemonth since, my face to the wind,
I laid by the sorrows of a year.

There's been another death: though by now
It has sunk under, like the water
Of small snow that fell the day I heard.
Once again (though to remember them
Is an ice along the skull) I call

To mind the gradually dying
Who haunt, more accusing than the dead,
These days I riffle at another
Year's end. Month by month I have screened
Their lives from mine; today each mindful hurt

That love inflicts in fostering love,
Each mindless act of chronic neglect
That dismembers a friendship alive,
I would undo. In exact patterns,
Yet frantic as drowners, apple-trees

Lift bare arms into the shortest day.
I'll not see them bud, burst into leaf,
Bloom, or their limbs bend when summer dust
Falls: my road leads by and beyond them.
Behind me somebody slides the door

And I turn and stare blank in a blank
Hangar. An appalling fragrance spills.
I breathe apples in before I see them,
Laxtons and Coxs, rack upon rack,
Shocking as a wiped-out flock of birds.

Ivy

Nine years ago I killed the ivy:
But once more it swarms the ancient wall
Round my plot. It has grown top-heavy
And rank, too much for the bricks to bear;
Powdery mortar has begun to fall

As fall it did our first winter here,
Eaten away by ravaging roots.
Ripened, the poison berries cluster;
Black swags in the February wind
Loom over my soil. A sleet shower starts

As I place the ladder, climb high and
Straddle the coping. Evergreen leaves
Conceal dust of dead seasons. I find
The wren's nest we hunted for one spring;
A ball; a lost doll that falls in halves

In my hands. Engrossed now, clambering
On, I incise with new secateurs
The tangle of years. Dismembering
Thick, reptilian stems, my palm bleeds;
I grasp sticky lushness. For the hours

It takes to shear clean my fifty yards
Of masonry, all is forgotten
Of what gnaws my present self. Last birds –
Rooks and lapwings – fly above a house
That once was not mine, will not be mine

One day; unfamiliar, those windows
Lit one by one and uncurtained yet
Against the dark. Another nine years,
Another, someone must grub up trunks
As I tomorrow shall in the wet

Field outside the wall. A blunted axe
He'll bring back, whoever he may be.
As long as I hone its edge. I'll give thanks
For the task. Duly, as men have done
Their several times each century

Since the bricks were laid, one morning soon
I'll re-point the gaps creepers have picked
Between them. I'll watch my ivy burn,
Tendrils of flame clinging to the flat
Surfaces of night; will sense what hacked

Vines will grip again, cannot be kept out.

Stanzas for the Graves

Rain had eased, an end-of-summer rain
Over Wales. Soon the sheened chapel roof,
Its wet slate tinctured like a rubbed plum,
Would dull, drying back into its bloom.
Day's lustre drained as late afternoon

Entered evening. Bringing autumn flowers,
Jagged dahlias, we trod coarse gravel
Away from laughter – stubbed cigarettes
And jokes while my friend spent his minutes
With dead kin, people I never knew.

The way was hard from the iron gate.
Marauding bracken and ripe blackberries
Stifled paths among forgotten graves
And graves half-forgotten, where black leaves
Rotted in sundry vessels chosen

With special care not so long ago.
I was a total stranger. No one
Lay in this ground to whom I might owe
My tepid, my true, my trumped-up awe,
Respect, remorse, or plain, wholesome love;

A neutral I came, shy guest without
Acquaintance at a party. I stood
Apart against an awkward headstone.
With nowhere to sit, to be alone,
I stared out over the pocked valley

Where nobody at that moment chose
To hang out washing, wheel a barrow
Of tools from a garden shed. I said
I'd fetch water. And as I half slid,
Half fell, scrambling down amid the crush

And clamour of these who wore their names
Like delegates at a convention,
I learned their ages, knew who loved whom
For how long and how much. Not for them
Had I felt pain of loss; but neither

Could I accord them that indifference
With which so casually I snub
Unimpinging billions of the quick.
I turned the tap on full, rubbed the muck
From a glass jar, filled it to the brim.

For all those who cannot be disowned,
Whose lives have not been marked with costly
Marble, I remember, with this, how
Strident were the flowers as the dusk grew
Around us. But not for them alone

I make my elegy. Imminent
Dead, you whom I love negligently,
Often hurt, and sometimes disremember,
Know how as we left for the umber
Dark, I saw all your eyes, alive as stars.

Elegy for an Old Acquaintance

Give sorrow words: the grief that does not speak
Whispers the o'erfraught heart, and bids it break.

(*Macbeth*, IV, iii)

Before true autumn the sun
    has less than warmth of flesh
and the days fall golden-green
    as the smooth rind of quinces;
to face into such sunlight
    is like bathing in milk.

And yet we have no name for
    the year's blandest interim
before the breath turns rancid
    in the mouth of October,
while the hours pour languidly
    upon themselves like oils.

Nor, as I hear you are dead,
    sometime, casual friend, have I
words for what is less than grief
    but more than common sorrow.
All our lives we prepare
    for the vaster bereavements:

every day, in case they die,
    I kill my children in my mind.
But no time is apt for the death
    of those we owe almost love –
a liking beyond affection;
    of those we seldom visit

but are always glad to see.
    Our stored tears are not for them
whose lives are but particles,
    not masonry of our own.
Their elegies are for ourselves,
    our parings, our bits of dead
skin. It is a nameless season
    of small mourning the heart keeps

every day that comes. I would wish
    to name its tart fruits of regret:
whatever it is we feel, making
    acknowledgment of minor loss,
of meagre failure, of yielding
    to time what was ours for good;

what shall we call those calendars
    of all unmemorable decay?
Old friend, if I speak no grief,
    yet know I am not untouched
by what you do so untimely.
    They are yours, the small, final

roses opening scentless in my garden.
    I spend an empty afternoon
watching the summer's end; this air
    I breathe from the quenched stubble-
fires fusts on the lung. It is for all
    us living, inarticulate, small

sorrowers my heart lurches now
    as I gag towards the sun;
for us all notice the lichen
    on the wall bounding what is mine
and sense what feeble, savage-rooted growths
    pick at the fabric of happiness.

After the Funeral

for William Plomer, d. September 21st 1973

Home once more to a parched garden so sparse of flowers
It seems winter. The rose pergola bears one bud;
Here, good-humouredly, you chaffed my untidiness
Once, years back. It is hard, thinking of you as dead,

You now dumb. For the first time it is you not I
Who owe letters. I'll have, somehow, to do without
Your old-fashioned and unphonable presence who
Could be written to nights, mornings of blank despair

When no voice may be heard bearably answering back.
And, moreover, to whom now shall I send by post
Hard pears, Portuguese quinces and the home-made jams
You so savoured? Your heart stopped at the time of year

When fruit falls to the lawn harvested not by hand
But wind, cold, and a first frost that the tiring stem
Must yield to; when the great men in their severalty –
Casals, Auden, Neruda – would be taken, too.

Not young men: but their lives' work, unaccomplished quite,
Lies abandoned – a spade thrust in the earth, and left.
Now my garden's a lament for the makers. Small,
Red-brown, colour of blood days old, chrysanthemums

Turn tight buds to the sun. Tendrils of summer warmth
Clasp October; the leaves cling that you saw unfurl.
Not your elegy, this, William: it's much too soon.
Come year's ending, I'll mourn not for myself, but you.

Between Acts

Worthing, the nineties; pier and promenade
Busy with bathchairs, wicker bassinets.
An upper window in the Esplanade
Releases smoke of scented cigarettes.

In this lacklustre town a masterpiece
Takes shape. Elsewhere, with all the earnestness
Of being unimportant, grim police
Take evidence. So does a mad marquess.

But play, as well as The Play, must go on.
In a hired boat, and 'rented' for the day,
The author dallies down to Littlehampton.

So, bathing in fame and briny on the way,
Hubristic yet, and yet to be reviled,
Sails Oscar Fingall O'Flahertie Wills Wilde.

Wild Strawberries

They grew where no one
ever went but you
looking for something
else or for nothing
but some place beyond
places that you knew.

Sudden in fresh grass
you found them buried
alive in shadow
but ripening somehow
in the shade's stray warmth
where they chose to be.

At first they were few
as a baby has
little fingernails
and when you picked them
they lay on your palm
moments, finishing.

Sometimes there were more
but never enough
and year after year
you would come too soon
or late to find them
where they were before;

and those you tasted
ever afterwards
were only merest
evanescences
of those first berries
in a far-off wood

where your children go
in search of nothing
but what might be there
till the nights draw in
beyond the places
they know you know.

Gardener

New Year's Eve (a shag rug
the lawn, coarse with hoar-frost), rooks
spread wide wings in his emptied apple-trees.
They lift when he scares them

and caw, raucous, over the lily-pool.
Wafer ice is locking the apple-leaves
to tossed bundles, wads of dead feathers
after a rook-shoot.

All he'd wish this wintertide
is one more harvest, the barrowloads
he'd wheel back of another autumn's
superabundance.

Plots, look, are double-dug, pruning's done,
sleet blossoms into snow. Blunted light
in the creosote shed picks tools
lavished with Vaseline

tidy for spring. The floor stinks of fish-meal,
oil seeps from the power-mower. He longs
for the scent of clean, fresh-broken soil,
plunges a fist into

pressed moss peat that would burst from the bale.
Months must pass before next planting,
trowel and trug be draped with cobweb
and catalogues

keep from damp in orderly columns the seeds
he'll buy in due season. For the used earth
rests. Its limed clods will slide at the thaw
to crumble to tilth

in its own good time. Nothing, now, to tend
but bonfires. Today he crafts with tarred cord,
grease-bands. He smears, ties tight each bole,
while he remembers

windfalls, waspy, softening in the marigolds
where, also, the cricket ball fell
evening by evening till final summer collapsed
toward October.

His crops were ready, that first fall night.
Lifted potatoes in scattered patterns lay
through the dark to dry. In sacks he grappled them
muscular as wrestlers,

flung spent haulms to the yellowing pit.
Then: curds of cauliflower felt his knife,
ungloved were the fleshed broad beans, peas
rolled into colanders

and the kitchen busied. Kilner-jars stacked,
brim-packed with peaches and blackberries;
acrid in boiled vinegar, specked vegetables
browned into chutney;

red-currants, plums quobbled in the jam-kettle;
rhubarb and spinach bricked up the deep-freeze;
boxes crammed, ponderous the Conference pears
in tissue-paper.

And, as suddenly, the glut was done. Freed,
his pullets scratched and pecked all he'd missed.
The last Bramley picked, he replaced the ladder,
forked out the hen-house.

May cold sweeten the crudded litter, rain
leach it down. One more fortnight of surfeit
surely will come: enough to serve his own,
stuff to give away,

some that must waste or feed the wild birds.
He stares up, beyond his twigs, beyond his rooks
past space he is patient will brighten from solstice
into equinox.

Logs

Dumped from the truck, they
clobber onto themselves,
drum the outhouse walls
like yobs using boots.

Won't stack. I leave them
where they lie, my gnarls,
loppings, muddied chunks
and roots of a grubbed-up orchard.

Off-cuts, my father burns:
batten, deal, mahogany,
tongue-and-groove flooring.
From the way he warms himself

you can tell what a man is.
(Close, in a Tory park,
cord-wood dries for gentlemen;
stumps of elegant beeches

whiff like proffered snuff.)
To my hearth I carry smashed
kindling, crotched twigs.
Among the month-soft ashes

there are chars, knobby rusks.
Grudged, each flame I coax
from the load of rough fruitwood
tipped by today's gypsy;

any heat is won with skill,
stealth, furious bellows.
Late night, my fire shifts;
while I sleep, lyrically

flarings waste in an empty room.
I dread my craft, crabbed
words obdurate as sodden
bark: yet love the morning

scent of pear, the smoulder.
I might uncrumple a draft,
squatting at the grate the way
my father does. He holds

open hands to the bits
that catch, left of his labour.
I rake the slats of the fire-basket
for whatever embers, glad.

Barn Owl

When it flies
it's as if
an owl shape
of chaff
had lifted off
floursacks

to sift
over straw
where shrews are
velvet shred
not far from
the barn-loft

where it will
unwinnow
afterwards
falling through
roof-ties and rafters
behind those eyes.

sliding, pour themselves through themselves,
bits of miniature rivers.

Slack else, still
as worry beads left where they fell,

they abrade the young year's sun
in grit, green, brick, stucco brown,

a crumble. Always the eyes, coppery red –
sometimes the tongue, loose threads

flickering the wind.
This one I found

dead today, coils in a coil,
fills its Chinese bowl

with spent resilience. I'll keep it
as long as this takes to write.

Never before did I own a viper. Touch,
flinch,

to remember dry heaths of boyhood
summer, brackens, the sandy birchwood,

yelping in a pack for the hated snake –
deadlyadder. With a fork-ended stick

you'd fix his wriggling, knife his
sin. It was the lore of boys:

make a belt of the skin, heat
the flesh in an iron pan for the fat

that cures deafness.
Older, with a first girl in the sharp, dark grass,

you listened for the swift sibilance
of adders, appalled; and appalled in the silence

after, still you'd listen.
But, since, you've seen them often,

commonplace on an afternoon path,
exotic, arcane, tempting as death

to disturb. Several, zigzagged, ravelled as whips
lashed round themselves, whirls and loops,

finally subsided, a muddled tie-drawer.
One, disentangling, sloughed like a whore

peeling a stocking back. The new
head, mint as a pebble damped with dew,

had to be smashed. This one that's mine,
stiff in its small blood, its venom mine

for the simple milking, could kill
from posthumous spite. Did Adam, some residual

innocence left him in his great age,
lift the serpent's carcass in homage

to the nighthawk?
In the garden, to the dark

I commit this thing.
The fang

feels like red wire. I'd have
let this one live.

Creatures of a Zodiac

I
The ram

is his testicles. Will serve
a hundred ewes, easy. Fat

wethers blether wifeless on
the long moors, delectable,

soft as shawls; but he, apart,
accepts his special food. Tough

in his sour wool he grows old
and uneatable. Will butt,

from machismo, anyone
with tender hands. In autumn

he sets about his labour;
looks over his Roman nose,

selects where to begin. Thumps
in ramstam till it's done, black

scrotum tight with tottery lambs.

II
The bull

Hard as a wall of sandbags,
he fathers herds in test-tubes.

A man in a clean white coat,
satisfied, washes his hands;

like udders, the rubber gloves.
At market, lot 22

got dumped from a Land Rover:
bull calf, born of a milk breed,

useless. It fell on its knees
like a Muslim at prayer. I

bid my sentimental pound.
In sharp suits, pie-men guffawed

and the auctioneer yawned
while I led Plug through kingcups

to a pond to drink the moon.

III

The twins

Am one person divided
by two. Might have made something

of ourself, but for this curse.
Did not ask for a lifetime

of needing no mirror. One
laughs because the other laughs;

likewise, weeps. One day one will
die. Until then, in the first

person plural, I and I
continue to amuse you

with our ambiguity.
Sometimes we, too, cannot tell

who is who. Forget about
twin love. Our identity

is hateful as a triplet.

IV
The crab

Catch him in the coldest sea
(the North Sea, the coast of Maine)

and keep him cold. Above all
keep him alive when you get home,

with seaweed in a bucket.
Call up your friend. At table

provide brown bread-and-butter
and *sauce vinaigrette*; a crisp

salad, well-chilled Muscadet.
Covertly, you'll have removed

the dead-man's-meat. Serve the rest
on a platter of crushed ice.

Eat. Regale your guest with tales
of crabbing at dawn. Do not

mention pans, the scalded eyes.

V
The lion

Inside the safari park
(Worcestershire, Great Britain)

we reach an *al fresco* vault
containing gold, the great cats.

The steel grill clangs as a white
hunter warns us: all windows

to be kept tight shut. We move,
tailgating tailgating cars

in a long, slow raft. We are
cooped in airless Africa.

Nostalgic for Birmingham
inhaling deep through its bricks,

I glimpse a bit of a tree
draped with a marigold rug.

Afterwards, we'll buy postcards.

VI
The virgin

still knows what we cannot know
ever again. O children,

before carnality, how
was the world? You are other,

discrepant not only for
your youth. Old nuns have skin as

unused but creased as linen
long-forgotten in a drawer;

they would smell of lavender
in the grave. Not religion

makes their special sanctity,
not plain innocence yours. Flesh,

as soon as relevant, will
start to putrefy. We hold

holy what might have no end.

VII
The scales

An abomination, they
betoken parsimony.

God shall not be weighed. Sell me
stuff by the hunk, the armful.

Feed me in dollops. Exact
cooks lack the required panache:

great meals have no replica.
Avoid any man who deals

in micrograms, for he's up
to no good. Balance with hands.

As a rule of thumb, mice go
two to the ounce: lacking mice,

use judgment. A good judge will
toss in the guilty man's pan

a scrinch more of clemency.

VIII
The scorpion

Believe none of the legends.
If ringed with fire, it will not

sting itself to death. It will
die skittering with its fright,

flailing to the last, the way
humans do. Do not believe

it has no enemy. One
is dismembered in seconds

by army ants; with relish
it is gobbled down alive

by natives of Algeria.
Believe only (emptying

your shoes in Durango) that
Jove raised one to heaven: for

how else did Orion die?

IX

The archer

Sunday morning. A public
park, behind the tennis court.

Behold the bourgeoise figure
practising toxophily.

She is as old as England.
Fibre-glass flexes. She aims.

Her green person is bedecked
with thongs. Inside that leathery

head are fletchings, fistmeles, nocks.
Fifteen-forty on the court,

the server winds. A jackdaw
blows like a paper bag off

the cricket pavilion. Gold
equals Agincourt, Crécy.

Whizz. Thwock. Game, set and match.

X

The goat

Great-uncle kept a nanny
tethered to his damson tree.

She gave a gallon a day.
You'd drink some, warm, from a mug

made for the king's Jubilee.
We led her (when she'd be led)

by her chain to the churchyard.
Great-uncle was the sexton.

No sense taking a sickle,
he said, to grass that could spoil

in the summer rain. And so
we drank from grandfather's grave

and from *his* father's father's.
The milk was sweet. Sour damsons

fell when she butted the trunk.

XI
The water-carrier

I am required and always
shall be while men move ever

from springs of purest water.
Beyond where there are flowers

they glance up at my coming.
Though they are glad to see me,

let no one think I am loved.
They grudge the small pence I ask.

I am working against God
Who intended waterless

places. No one pays for spilth.
My shoulders are forever

raw from the rub of the yoke.
Shall I be damned? It is worth

more than souls to slake deserts.

XII
The fish

Is it limblessness makes them
alien? Sometimes they will touch,

with bellies deft as chiffon,
some swimmer come to their midst.

They move, lissom, from nowhere
to nowhere. For them there is

no unnecessary death;
they do not get left to bleed.

They are unaspiring, like
all finished things. God's perfect

artifacts, they need evolve
no more. (Though, could they grip with

more than their mouths, what cities
might rise from the sea?) They do

not know they cannot be mad.